Penguin Books

W9-COU-083

100 Ways to Calm the Crying

Pinky McKay is the author of *Sleeping Like a Baby*, *Toddler Tactics* and *Parenting By Heart*.

As an International Board Certified Lactation Consultant (IBCLC) and certified infant massage instructor, she works 'hands on' with parents and babies and writes for *Practical Parenting Magazine* and various national and international publications and websites including *Littlies* magazine (New Zealand), *Kindred*, Bellybelly, Bubhub, Motherinc and Kidslife.

As a mother and grandmother, Pinky has a wealth of first-hand experience and loads of empathy for parents whose heartstrings are torn by the wails of an unsettled baby.

Pinky can be contacted through her website at www.pinkymckay.com.au

100 Ways to Calm the Crying

PINKY McKAY

Penguin Books

PENGUIN BOOKS

Published by the Penguin Group
Penguin Group (Australia)
250 Camberwell Road, Camberwell, Victoria 3124, Australia
(a division of Pearson Australia Group Pty Ltd)
Penguin Group (USA) Inc.
375 Hudson Street, New York, New York 10014, USA
Penguin Group (Canada)
90 Eglinton Avenue East, Suite 700, Toronto, Canada ON M4P 2Y3
(a division of Pearson Penguin Canada Inc.)
Penguin Books Ltd
80 Strand, London WC2R 0RL England
Penguin Ireland
25 St Stephen's Green, Dublin 2, Ireland
(a division of Penguin Books Ltd)
Penguin Books India Pvt Ltd
11 Community Centre, Panchsheel Park, New Delhi – 110 017, India
Penguin Group (NZ)
67 Apollo Drive, Rosedale, North Shore 0632, New Zealand
(a division of Pearson New Zealand Ltd)
Penguin Books (South Africa) (Pty) Ltd
24 Sturdee Avenue, Rosebank, Johannesburg 2196, South Africa

Penguin Books Ltd, Registered Offices: 80 Strand, London, WC2R 0RL, England

First published by Lothian Books, 2002
This revised edition published by Penguin Group (Australia), 2008

1 3 5 7 9 10 8 6 4 2

Text copyright © Pinky McKay 2002, 2008

Cover design by Claire Wilson © Penguin Group (Australia)
Text design by Karen Trump © Penguin Group (Australia)
Cover photograph by Veer
Typeset in 10/16 New Aster by Post Pre-press Group, Brisbane, Queensland
Printed and bound in Australia by McPherson's Printing Group, Maryborough, Victoria

National Library of Australia
Cataloguing-in-Publication data:

McKay, Pinky, 1952–
100 ways to calm the crying / author, Pinky McKay.
Camberwell, Vic. : Penguin, 2008.
9780143009177 (pbk.)
Crying in infants.
Infants – Care.
Newborn infants – Care.
One hundred ways to calm the crying

649.122

penguin.com.au

To my own 'Velcro' babies, and to parents
of crying babies everywhere

Author's note: Because children come in both genders, I have alternated the terms 'she' and 'he' throughout the book. No sexism intended – boys and girls have equal ability to tickle your funny bone or pluck at your heartstrings, and as babies they are equally delicious.

In some of the personal stories, the names of parents and children have been changed to protect their privacy.

Contents

Chapter five

Chapter six

Chapter seven

Foreword

Here is a book that is down-to-earth, warm and – unlike many other books that deal with crying – *respects* babies.

Crying babies often seem aliens in our midst. We interpret their distress as hostile and feel helpless when we try to communicate with creatures who don't speak our language and certainly haven't read the same parenting books.

Some systems of baby management are bossy, manipulative and, quite honestly, bullying methods of dealing with a baby's unhappiness by training it as if it were a puppy.

This book is quite different.

There is an art in observing a baby and learning to speak this new little person's language. We do this when we hold and cradle, stroke and rock babies, sing and talk to them, are aware of their responses and gradually become skilled in communicating with them. When this happens, we develop confidence.

As you read these pages, bear in mind that having a crying baby is often treated as a private matter, something a mother has to sort out for herself. In the end it is usually she who is expected to cope. She is blamed when her baby cries – and it is often taken for granted that she must be an inadequate mother.

But the personal is the political. Each inconsolably crying baby is evidence that the transition to motherhood in our culture is made difficult because women are isolated from each other and have little emotional or practical support during this major life transition.

The challenge is for us to reach out to each other, mutually validating our experiences, and work to create a society that actively nurtures mothers and babies.

Sheila Kitzinger
Oxford
April 2002

Introduction

You are walking the floor with a crying baby – and tears are streaming down your face too. Why can't I comfort my baby? you wonder. Am I losing my milk? Is he sick? Why am I crying as well? Could I have postnatal depression? Perhaps your partner is looking at you, feeling equally helpless, which makes you somehow feel even more inadequate. And if he is not at home with you but at work, you might experience feelings ranging from loneliness to resentment – that he has the easy job.

It is little wonder that you feel overwhelmed when your baby cries: apart from having a natural physiological response to your little one's distress, you probably feel as though you have just fallen, at the deep end, into a complex and unpredictable new job that you have absolutely no training for and which has no clearly defined job spec. You have exchanged smart black business suits for tracksuits – not least because for a while nothing else fits – and now you are being wept or weed on several times a day. You have gone from eating lunch in restaurants in civilised style to juggling a baby and a fork as you endeavour to access a mouthful of food that your partner has had to chop into pieces for you. Or even worse, you need two hands to dance the colic waltz or rock a crying baby who won't be consoled by a milky 'bust in the mouth', so your partner actually has to poke food into *your* mouth (there isn't a single erotic connotation here!) Or you are home alone, so you eat cold food. Again!

As modern parents, you and your partner have most likely planned this baby down to the finest details – even perhaps to the last tick of the biological clock. Now you have discovered that you can't slot a baby into a 2 p.m. appointment in your organiser – in fact, a large part of your day is spent trying to organise the logistics of a dash to the local shops in between feeds, sleeps and wails, just to buy a loaf of bread. Perhaps you didn't even make it into the tracksuit today: your baby has spent so much of the time crying that you are still in your dressing-gown, still sitting in the same chair you were in when your partner left for work – for the *real* world – this morning. After a few more days of this, you will be crying more than your baby.

From my hands-on work with parents, I know that many feel overwhelming pressure to have a 'good' baby: a baby who sleeps, eats and smiles, preferably to some predetermined, socially acceptable schedule – certainly not a crying baby. Many have told me they are afraid to speak openly about how their babies behave: those whose infants don't simply feed, play and sleep (preferably in that order) often feel as though they are somehow abnormal if they 'give in' to their baby's cries; mothers whose babies fail sleep school fear that they too have failed as they secretly soothe little night howls; and many mothers exist in isolation because they are afraid of the stares and advice they will attract if they venture out in public with a bawling baby.

Although much of the pressure put on parents (often by themselves) is related to their baby's sleep patterns – or lack of them – there would be much less concern about sleep if these babies were apparently happy. Having a crying baby is so stressful, yet practical information about this aspect of parenting is scarce. While there is a plethora of information about getting babies to sleep, many authors actually recommend that parents leave their babies to cry. *100 Ways to Calm the Crying* is my response to those desperate, confused parents who have contacted me in their search for ways to soothe and connect with their babies. Some of their personal stories are included in this book, along with gentle ways to calm the crying – day *and* night. There is also advice about caring for yourself and your relationship as you struggle through a blur of sleepless nights and difficult days – from current research and from 'experts' including both professionals and parents, for after all parents are the practitioners who know firsthand how a baby's tears tug at your heartstrings. And, because crying babies are not limited to first-time parents (my own crying baby was our *third* child), I have also included some strategies for maintaining sibling harmony.

Just as each parent and each family is different, your baby is a unique little being. So my aim is to show you how to read *your* baby's cues and to listen to *your* baby, rather than applying one-size-fits-all strategies that require either you or your baby to do the fitting. Listen to your child, listen to your heart and choose the information that suits you both. Above all, remember that your baby's cries are a form of communication: his only form of communication in fact, and not a reflection of your parental skills. Enjoy the moments of calm between cries and when the going gets tough just repeat the mantra, 'This too shall pass.' It will, all too soon. I promise.

Chapter one
The crying game

The first rule of the crying game is, 'Don't blame yourself.' It is not your fault if your baby cries – even when she cries and cries! According to a 1996 study at the University of London, crying is not attributable to inadequate parenting, to obstetric complications, to breast- or bottle-feeding, to birth order or to gender. Crying is your baby's language. At first, it is pretty much the only way an infant can express feelings like discomfort, hunger, exhaustion and loneliness. It is also the only way she can release pent-up stress. As your baby grows she will learn other ways to communicate: through facial expressions and body language generally, and eventually by telling you *exactly* how she feels and what she needs.

We all know that babies cry, and we know it long before we have one of our own. Even so, the reality of a crying baby up close and very personal can challenge all our preconceptions about parenthood and our own coping skills. Discovering just how much love and care a baby actually needs, how unpredictable babies' needs are, and how your baby's cry will almost unfailingly pierce you to the core, is an enormous shock to many parents.

'Before becoming parents, we were warned that a baby cries. Intellectually we understood this, but how was I to know that not only do they cry when they are hungry, but they cry for a dozen other reasons too. And the big shocker: a baby plays, gets tired and then goes to sleep doesn't it? No one ever talked at length about how difficult my baby would find it to get to sleep.

'You don't simply hear a baby cry – as if that isn't heart and gut wrenching enough – the surprise to me was that you feel your own baby cry in every single cell of your body. (I don't use a monitor – I think I'd feel him crying across the other side of the country!)

'The good news is that over time, you really do get to know what is a grizzle, what is frustration; hunger; needing a cuddle; a fright; illness; pain; or tiredness.

'I am a changed being in motherhood – always on high alert: my baby's crying is my cue to respond, and every single day each tear makes more sense as we continue our journey getting to know each other.'

Fiona, mother of one

Many of us have mixed feelings about crying, and our culture reinforces this response. Consider how comfortable you feel listening to a friend who is sobbing. How comfortable are you with expressing your own feelings openly? Would you feel somehow weak or incompetent if you shed a tear (or perhaps a flood of tears) in public – at work, for instance? Where do you find yourself crying? Alone, behind closed doors? Many of us have learned early in life that crying is unacceptable – or at least that it causes discomfort to the people around us.

'I can remember, when I was a child, being teased for crying. Adults used to say things like, "The more you cry, the less you pee." Or I would be told, "Stop that or I'll give you something to really cry about!" Now, I cry in the shower. I don't share my tears.'

Sally, mother of three

With such strong messages, it is perfectly natural to feel anxious and tense, or even guilty, when your baby cries. And it is normal for these feelings in turn to affect the way you react to your baby's wails.

Get real

When the baby you expected isn't the baby you have in your arms (well, not for most of the day at least), it is easy to beat up on yourself and wonder what you are doing wrong. But this probably means that you had unrealistic expectations. Babies come with varying temperaments and very individual needs. Babies cannot be scheduled like a bus timetable or a day of business appointments: they are individuals – just like us! Most babies are likely to need an *average* of nine hours' basic care each day (which, of course, includes the night-time as well) and most babies, just like most of us, need some extra nurturing from time to time.

'For the first eight weeks my baby cried all day. At first I could often settle her, but by three weeks there was nothing that would really work for more than a minute or two for most of the day. I had read all the books, tried everything in the "settling" books. My days were spent rocking, patting, massage, dancing with her to "Midnight Train to Georgia" (this one was about the most reliable and I have a 90-minute tape which is just this song, over and over), wearing her in the Baby Bjorn (worked sometimes), everything. The only way I could take a shower

some days was to have one foot out of the shower rocking Caitlin in her rocker. My diet consisted of toast, apples and cereal bars – all things I could eat with one hand. I felt like a failure as a mother, and I felt terribly sorry for my baby because she only had me, not a "better" mother.'

Rachel, mother of one

'In the sleep-deprived state of shock in those first few weeks, I was convinced he was crying because he hated me. "Good" mothers had contented little babies who never cried, but instead sent telepathic messages to their carers to alert them to their needs!'

Chrissy, mother of one

'Jack was never a really consistent sleeper, in the sense that he was a very alert and wakeful baby during the day: he was very content to have little power naps, only to be awake again in 45 minutes ready to play. I can now see on reflection, that he was satisfying his individual needs – but in my exhaustion, I allowed others to convince me that if he had more sleep, my life would get easier. So, from about a week after he was born, I became obsessed with him sleeping for long periods of time. I would be disappointed if he "failed" to reach at least an hour, but would be bursting with pride if he slept for three to four

hours. I equated how well he slept with how good a mother I was.'

Cherie, mother of one

1 Be prepared: The fact is that most babies are likely to need an average of nine hours' basic care each day (which, includes the night-time as well) and most babies, just like most of us, need some extra nurturing from time to time.

Why babies cry

A baby cries because she needs something – or someone. She is saying, 'I don't feel right. Please help me.' Sheila Kitzinger explains: 'Imagine being stuck, helpless, inside a plastic box, unable to move much, to get food or a drink when you are hungry or thirsty, or do anything for yourself, and being expected to lie there, in solitary confinement, staring at the ceiling. The only thing you can do to change what happens around you is to make a very loud noise.' It is useful to understand some of the reasons why babies do cry, so that you know that *your* baby's cries – especially if she cries a lot – aren't somehow a reflection of your incompetence or a sign of rejection. Indeed, some professionals claim that crying is a normal and important aspect of infant development. Here are some of the reasons babies cry:

- **physical:** hunger, discomfort, a wet or dirty nappy, pain (see the chapters 'Is she hungry' and 'Little pains')
- **emotional:** feeling lonely, overtired, bored, frustrated, afraid – including separation anxiety (these topics are addressed throughout the book) and to release pent-up stress or tension
- **environmental:** sensitivity to loud noises and bright lighting, excessive stimulation (see 'Womb service', page 35 and 'Solving the sleep puzzle', page 128)
- **developmental:** there are a number of emotional, physical and neurological stages that cause upheaval and anxiety in babies (see 'Crying times', page 13)

Temperament is also a factor that affects how much babies cry. Some babies, for example, find it more difficult than others to block out stimulation, or to move smoothly from sleeping to waking (and vice versa). Again, this is not a result of the way you handle your baby. In fact, paediatrician William Sears coined the label 'high-needs baby' to emphasise that such behaviours are a factor of the baby's temperament and reaction to her environment rather than inappropriate care by the parent. Research also suggests that some babies simply cry more than others: a study into foetal movements revealed traits akin to temperament which can predict how much individual babies are likely to cry.

Crying spells in the evening are so universal that this behaviour has also been labelled by 'experts' – mothers, that is – as the 'arsenic hour' or the 'witching hour': this is the time of day when mothers, at the end of their own energy reserves, generally have to contend with the combination of cooking dinner, a partner (or themselves) arriving home from work, and possibly the needs of other tired and hungry children, as well as a crying baby. It seems that even in cultures where babies have continual close contact with their mothers and ready access to the breast, and rarely cry during the day, it is quite common for them to cry for long periods in the evening.

It is fairly commonly accepted by both parents and professionals that babies reach a 'crying peak' at around six weeks. The University of London study concluded that a developmental process causes most babies to cry more at six weeks: it also found that premature babies get grizzly at about the time they would have been six weeks old and, apparently, even babies in so-called primitive cultures also have a six-week grizzle. Changes such as those outlined under 'Crying times' below can be quite confusing to a baby as her familiar world is suddenly turned upside-down.

> **2**   *Your baby's cries – especially if she cries a lot – are not somehow a reflection of your competence (or lack of it) or a sign of rejection.*

Crying times

As well as the six-week crying peak, there are several major developmental stages during the first twelve months that may unsettle babies. Just as babies have physical growth spurts, their brains grow more rapidly during the first year of life than at any other time, doubling in volume and reaching 60 per cent of adult size by the end of that twelve months. Neurological studies have shown that dramatic changes take place in the brains of babies and children at certain points, shortly after which they experience a marked leap forward in learning and mental development. According to Dutch researchers Hetty Van de Rijt and Professor Frans Plooij, all babies go through at least seven of these developmental leaps in the first year of life. Although calmer babies cope with these stages relatively easily, in others confusion, frustration and anxiety may make them so unsettled that they cling to the only safety and security they know – you!

It may help to photocopy the following list of developmental 'leaps' and post it on your refrigerator as a reminder that your little one's unsettled spells may be due to normal physiological changes.

6 weeks: Around this time, significant sensory and digestive changes take place. They are more awake and alert, breathe more regularly, cry real tears for the first time, startle and tremble less often. They express their likes and dislikes more frequently and are more interested in their surroundings. Babies commonly experience a growth spurt at this time and require more frequent feeds for a few days.

8 weeks: Big changes in the way babies experience their senses. They see, hear, smell and taste in a way that's completely new to them and this can make them feel puzzled, confused and upset. They may be fascinated by patterns and light, listen more keenly to sounds, and discover their hands and feet. They may be more wary of strangers, want you to keep them occupied, sleep badly, lose their appetite, suck their thumb more.

12 weeks: Babies are able to co-ordinate their move-oments much more smoothly, are more perceptive about changes taking place in their environment, notice people's comings and goings. There may be another bout of shyness, sleeping badly, not wanting to feed but wanting to suck a great deal.

19 weeks: Their ability to understand the world around them becomes more developed. They begin to grasp that the world is made up of objects that continue to exist when out of their sight. They may get clingy again.

26 weeks: Babies can perceive distance between objects, and will climb up to reach things. They also understand about the distance between themselves and their mother, where previously they didn't perceive themselves as separate from their mother. They may be more fearful.

37 weeks: Babies recognise categories of things. They experiment with foods and toys, and want you to play constantly.

46 weeks: Babies begin to see things in sequence and string events together. This means they can now make associations like, 'Here comes the babysitter: that means Mummy will be going out' (so they may cry in anticipation of being left).

Babies do, of course, vary in the speed at which they

reach these developmental milestones, but the point is that there is a lot going on in your baby's inner world that may not be obvious to you. So, just as your baby may need more feeds to satisfy an appetite increase during a growth spurt (see the chapter 'Is she hungry?'), she may also at times need extra support to help her cope with frustration and confusion at times of developmental change. It is logical, too, that babies' patterns of behaviour (for which read 'sleeping' and 'feeding') alter to match each new phase.

Separation anxiety

Around six months is the beginning of an important developmental process known as 'separation anxiety': this commonly lasts from the time babies realise you are a separate being until around eighteen months when they understand that when you disappear you will come back.

It is also normal for toddlers and older children to experience episodes of separation anxiety. The best way to deal with this is to help your little one feel secure by responding to her cries for reassurance. And if you do have to leave her with a carer, be honest and say goodbye: it is helpful to have a farewell ritual as well as a return greeting, so she can learn that although you leave her sometimes you will always come back. Even though she will probably yell as you leave, if you sneak away she will become distrustful and clingy, which means more crying in the long run. Usually, if you have been honest, babies settle quite quickly if they are familiar with their carers.

'My son has just started day care at age two, for one day a week. On the night after his first day he wanted me to stay with him while he went to sleep and it took him some time to get to sleep. I sat by him quietly but I was there – he had been separated from me and needed this comfort. As he gets used to the centre he will no longer need that every time, but for the three-quarters of an hour it took him to go off to sleep while I sat by his bed to give him that security I could have done dishes, cleaned up, had a shower or got on the computer; I could have said "No" and many parents would think it justifiable. However, I could not do that, as I knew he needed comfort.'

Rhonda, mother of a two-year-old

3 *If you do have to leave her with a carer, be honest and say goodbye: it is helpful to have a farewell ritual as well as a return greeting, so she can learn that although you leave her sometimes, you will always come back.*

Comforting will *not* spoil your baby!

As the parent of a crying baby, you will be sure to hear (and be pressured to believe) well-meant rationalisations such as 'Crying won't hurt her' or 'You don't want to spoil her.' Sometimes it may also be implied that you can 'teach' your baby to behave conveniently (that is, to cry less and sleep more) if only you are persistent enough. This approach is often couched in the language of the power struggle ('controlled crying', 'controlled comforting', 'parent-directed feeding') and soon it becomes all too easy to see your baby's cries as manipulation rather than communication.

'It's just so frustrating not knowing what to do when your baby cries and you know he is fed, clean and the only factor (I think) is tiredness. Well-intentioned people – just this morning on the phone – can hear him crying in the background, and when you say, "I was cuddling him," back comes the reply, "Well, you've created a rod for your own back now!"

'Where does the guilt come from, as I watch his tears and screams subside as a quick cuddle in my arms does the trick? Should I not be feeling satisfied that I have the magic touch?'

Helen, mother of a three-month-old

'It is our most basic parenting philosophy to always try to put ourselves in our children's place. For example, we ask ourselves, "How would we feel if we were left to cry alone to get to sleep each night?" It always amazes us that the "experts" suggest we let babies and young children, who are not yet able to understand, cry and to ignore the child's earliest attempts to communicate their needs to us. It doesn't seem to us like it sets up a good beginning to bonding and communicating in families. I have never really understood why in our culture we are in such a hurry to make our children fit into an adult lifestyle.'

Donna and Iain, parents of three

There is no sense at all in entering a power struggle with your baby over natural functions such as sleeping and eating. By not responding to her signals, the only things that are being 'spoilt' are your relationship with your baby and your own self-confidence. As your baby fails to fit the regime you are trying to impose, you feel more and more inadequate (and possibly angry). And, as you struggle to teach your baby that you are in control, she may also learn perhaps the saddest lesson of all: that she is helpless, that she has no power to communicate – so what is the use of trying?

4   There is no sense in entering a power struggle with your baby over natural functions such as sleeping and eating. By not responding to her signals, the only things that are being 'spoilt' are your relationship with your baby and your own self-confidence.

Your baby's cry has been designed for her survival and you are programmed to react. A mother's body chemistry changes when her baby cries: the blood flow to her breasts doubles and she has a hormone-induced urge to respond. When you attend to your baby promptly you not only get better at 'reading' her crying language but come to learn her pre-cry signals: wriggling, anxious facial expressions, little grimaces, flailing arms, 'rooting' at the breast (when you touch her cheek, she turns her head to that side in an attempt to grasp a nipple), changes in breathing, and little noises that say, 'I am working up to a cry.' You will be able to see when she is bored, frightened, hungry, tired or over-whelmed, and as you respond accordingly you will be able to avert full-blown crying.

In the early months, your baby's cry is automatic. If you leave her to cry, she is likely to become even more upset as her crying picks up momentum. And after a little while she won't even know why she was crying in the first place – she will just be crying because she can't stop, and so will be much harder to settle. If you are breastfeeding, it is particularly important to respond quickly to hunger cues: a baby who is left to work up to a full-blown cry will have a more disorganised suck and may have difficulty latching on correctly (because when she is yelling, her tongue will be up against the roof of her mouth), or she may only suck for a short time before she falls asleep with exhaustion.

Apart from draining your own precious energy, imposing strict feeding and sleep regimes have been linked to mothers' milk supplies dwindling and to a 'failure to thrive' in infants. It may also have longer-term consequences for mental health: there is emerging evidence that distress at being left to cry (abandonment) changes the physiology of the brain and may predispose children to stress disorders such as panic, anxiety and depression later in life. Paediatrician William Sears has commented that 'babies who are "trained" not to express their needs may appear to be docile, compliant or "good" babies. Yet, these babies could be depressed babies who are shutting down the expression of their needs. They become children who don't speak up to get their needs met and eventually become the highest-need adults.'

5   *If you leave her to cry, she is likely to become even more upset as her crying picks up momentum. And after a little while she won't even know why she was crying in the first place – she will just be crying because she can't stop, and so will be much harder to settle.*

So be assured that when your little one switches from tears to grins the moment you pick her up, this is not an indicator that she is a clever little schemer with a parent (you!) wrapped around her proverbial little finger, but rather a demonstration of her growing trust in you. And your responsiveness could even make your baby smarter: neuroscientists and clinicians have documented that loving interactions which are sensitive to a child's needs influence the way the brain grows and can increase the number of connections between nerve cells; and a recent US study found that when mothers responded appropriately to their babies' cries during the first month, these children had higher language and cognitive scores at eighteen months.

In the early months your baby simply isn't capable of deciding which kind of cry will get attention. She can't be 'spoilt' and she can't be 'taught' to wait for her needs to be met. In fact, research shows that babies who are attended to promptly during the first six months cry and whinge less in the next six months and even later – responding now could be cheap insurance against a demanding toddler!

> 'Kieran was unsettled from the word go; he rarely left my arms, sleeping only at the breast, in my arms, the Meh Tai or a moving pram. The disapproving mutters grew louder. I read again William Sears' book, The Fussy Baby – *it could have been written just for us. Kieran was a 'high-needs baby', and what we were doing was just right.*
>
> 'Kieran continued to breastfeed to sleep for longer than either of the girls had – things came to a head when he was eighteen months old. I declined to attend a family wedding because Kieran was not welcome. I was unwilling to leave him with my patient mother, who would not be able to settle him in the way that worked best. (Although later on she spent memorable evenings looking after Kieran and my also-breastfed niece, who was the same age, with all three of them asleep on the couch when we arrived home!)
>
> 'My husband, when discussing my decision with his mother, was told, "Kieran wouldn't be like this if she didn't carry him in that sling thing all the time"!'

Yvette, mother of three

'One thing that I found very difficult to handle was the almost persistent desire of others to see me "control cry" my baby. On one occasion, someone tried to convince me that babies "needed" to be left to cry in order to fully develop their chest muscles and rib cage for breathing! Whatever the reason for persuasion – the general consensus was that if I didn't adopt the technique of control crying then I was not deserving of any sympathy or support. I was the silly woman who insisted on cuddling, rocking, feeding my baby to sleep – surely I couldn't expect others who cared for him to do the same thing. What astounded me was that the biggest advocates for this practice were mothers themselves! Surely they too had felt the pain and anguish that I felt, on hearing their babies cry. Surely they too felt instinctively compelled to pick their babies up, to kiss them and rock them off to sleep. "No," they said. "It's for the best, you know – if we don't do this now, he'll never sleep through!" The look of total conviction on their faces when saying this has firmly convinced me that there is a certain level of psychological brainwashing that takes place at certain institutions alongside the wrapping and patting – they are slowly convincing women to turn away from their natural instinct to protect and love their baby out of fear of losing their identity. It's as though if they don't do it, the child will promise to be an irreparable rascal at the age of six weeks – destined to be hell bent on destroying their lives forever.

'I admit that in choosing not to leave my baby crying, I have sacrificed many hours of my life to his comfort. I have walked kilometres of carpet, fed him gallons of my milk, sang a multitude of songs and given an innumerable number of kisses and cuddles in the effort to make him feel loved and safe. At times my fatigue has been out of control and at times I have come close to breaking point. But when I look around at all the other mothers of children the same age, I hear and see the same experience regardless of their choice of parenting technique – all the mothers I know admit that parenting is hard work! I didn't choose to parent my child in this way out of any fixed idea of achieving anything in particular – I have just followed my heart and done what feels right to me as we travel down the path of life. I think what it ultimately comes down to is trust. I choose to put trust in my baby and his ability to tell me what he needs and I trust in my ability to hear these calls for help and act on them. Just think – if we were left to parent on our own with no "experts" or "baby books" to tell us what to do, all we would have left to act on would be this instinct. Since we have relied on this instinct for thousands of years to survive, surely it holds some strength of argument.'

Melinda, mother of a two-year-old

6 *Babies who are attended to promptly during the first six months cry and whinge less in the next six months and even later – responding now could be cheap insurance against a demanding toddler!*

Adjust your response as your baby grows

When your baby is around six months old she will learn a new sort of cry, called an 'intentional' cry. This means she has learnt that if she cries you will respond, and she will now cry to gain your attention. This is not a bad thing: the need for human interaction and/or stimulation is a legitimate one. A few years ago we were presented with tragic media images of orphaned Romanian babies lying motionless and malnourished in their cots. This is an extreme example, perhaps, but these institutionalised babies failed to thrive because they never learned the connection between their cries and a loving response.

However, although experts tend to agree that it is best to respond to your baby's cries promptly during the first six months, there is also a general consensus that as your baby grows it is equally important to foster her confidence in her own ability to do things for herself. This doesn't mean that you must suddenly change your parenting style and ignore your baby's cries, or force her to experience high levels of frustration so she learns to be independent. Rather it means continuing to observe your baby as you always have, and using your own intuition and wisdom, as well as your awareness of your baby's cues, to respond appropriately to a 'red alert' cry, a grizzle and tears of frustration. At this stage, you will be able to teach her gently that you are close but that perhaps she can wait a moment or two, and talk reassuringly to her until you reach her. One way to manage this is to bring baby into your world, rather than yours revolving totally around her. While she is a newborn, you can do this by carrying her in a sling as you work or put her on the floor near you so that she has space to discover her own body, to learn to roll and develop mobility. Later, as she becomes mobile and can amuse herself (of course, you may have to help her initiate play and you will need to baby-proof her environment), you can do your tasks nearby but still watch her closely. (I look at all this in more detail in the chapter 'Distractions and diversions'.)

If you are concerned about how much attention you should be showering on your baby, relax. Although it is a delicate balance, it is far better to err on the side of too much attention than to not meet her needs. You can gradually adapt your responses at any stage – you know your baby best.

> 'The dishes will wait, but Annalise will not want cuddles forever before it becomes "uncool". Our critics say we are doing the wrong thing and not letting her become independent. I say we are giving her the confidence to know we are there if we are needed. My question is how can it be wrong when it feels so right?'
>
> **Kristy, mother of a nine-month-old**

7 At around six months she learns that crying will gain your attention. At this stage, you can teach her gently that you are close but that perhaps she can wait a moment or two. One way to manage this is to bring baby into your world, rather than yours revolving totally around her.

A little advice goes a long way

Advice is never in short supply for the parents of a crying baby. Whenever your baby cries, you can be certain you'll encounter stares (if you are out and about), or comments (and even criticism) from perfect strangers as well as your nearest and dearest. Suddenly *everybody* is an expert about *your* baby!

'From about three weeks, Molly had a crying spell lasting up to two hours around midnight. A "good" friend came over to help one day when my husband and I were both ill. She commented, "My boy never cried without a reason, but your little girl just cries all the time. I wonder why?" If ever a statement was completely unnecessary for a brand new mum, that one was!'

Alex, mother of a five-month-old

'When Georgia, our first baby, was six weeks old we went from Sydney to Adelaide to stay with my parents. When we returned home to our tiny flat, our neighbours greeted us and asked if we had been away for a couple of weeks. "Yes, why?" we asked. Oh, they had noticed that "crying baby" wasn't crying! That's what they called her, they said, because she cried all the time. I was really hurt by those comments: it felt like they were criticising me for not making her stop, like there was something wrong with my precious baby. When their baby was born about a month later, I never told them I thought she cried a lot, but by then I had an almost-four-month-old who had settled right down and their baby cried a lot!'

Keren, mother of two

Trust your instincts

It is easy for others to tell you what to do, especially if it involves leaving your baby to 'cry it out' simply because it isn't *their* baby: your baby's cries don't pluck at other people's heartstrings the way they do at yours. And they aren't there at 3 a.m. listening to *your* baby. The truth is that no matter how tired, stressed, uncertain or inadequate you feel, you *do* know your baby best. So listen to your heart and listen to your baby. Trust the connection between you, and when you encounter negativity towards your parenting and/or your crying baby remember that by meeting your baby's needs and standing firm this connection will grow stronger and so will you.

'I am generally open to most pieces of advice and, like everyone, use what I think might help. Mostly, I find most pieces of advice help a little. Using your instinct is probably the best option as it boosts your confidence when it works.'

Sandy, mother of a six-month-old

'There is no foolproof way to get every child to calm down, and some children won't calm down no matter what you do. Just tell yourself that it is a sure sign of brilliance. Then hand them off to a grandmother and go shopping.'

Melissa, mother of two

Sometimes it isn't worth expending energy trying to convince your critics that you are the expert where your baby is concerned – it is better to conserve your energy for your baby. However, it is helpful to have some strategies to deal with criticism, rather than allowing other people to undermine your confidence and upset you (and your baby, who invariably picks up and mirrors your feelings).

8 *Sometimes it isn't worth expending energy trying to convince your critics that you are the expert where your baby is concerned – it is better to conserve your energy for your baby.*

Agree to disagree

How you respond to unwanted advice can be just as important as what you say. Although it can be difficult in the heat of the moment, if you tune in to where the other person is coming from it may be easier to turn a deaf ear to irrelevant advice. For example, bear in mind that, while babies' needs have remained the same, parenting styles have changed. Older people, including your parents, are likely to favour scheduling your baby's feeds and sleeps, and you may well hear, 'She's already spoilt!' as your baby's cries turn to smiles when you pick her up. In the same way, when they blame your baby's crying on wind, by all means let Grandma burp her till the cows come home – baby won't mind – just don't agree to funny old remedies like 'a drop of brandy on her dummy'.

You may find it helps to openly discuss the parenting information that has changed since you were a baby. Failing that, when Grandma – or anyone else – makes negative comments, try taking a deep breath and counting to ten (slowly). Or pretend you are standing next to a window: imagine opening the window and letting the comments simply blow away, then smile and say, 'Yes, and isn't she clever, she already knows we adore her?' Then pass them your little bundle – hopefully, they won't be able to resist her.

And do remember that you don't have to defend your actions to anyone. This is *your* baby: she is the only person you need to defend. Make eye contact and stand firm as you say, 'This works well for us,' or simply smile and say, 'When [*baby's name*] is happy, our whole family is happy.' It can even be a strategic advantage if you smile as you respond – your critics may think you are so away with the fairies that they will get off your case.

You can be sure to hear the word 'spoil' as you race to pick up your crying baby. This was what your mother was probably warned would happen to *you* if she dared to pick you up before four hours were up – and there's nothing wrong with you, is there? She probably also believes that babies have tempers – because once upon a time babies who didn't stop howling were described in those terms as the bedroom door was closed behind them. This is a difficult one to deal with, but if Grandma (or anyone else) doesn't respect your choice to respond to your baby, don't choose her as a babysitter. On the other hand, she may love cuddling her grandchild – after all, it's not her responsibility if you have a 'spoilt' child.

Don't forget, though, that the more information you have the greater your range of options. All advice is worth considering, so long as you choose carefully what suits you and your baby. When you are offered advice, you can just say something like, 'Thanks, I'll remember that,' then discard any irrelevant suggestions as you see fit.

'Ask questions of professionals, your parents, friends who are parents, grandparents, but be careful of the person giving you advice who has never had children. You can pick them a mile off, or should I say they will pick you a mile off and suggest everything from leaving them in a dark room to cry themselves to sleep, to giving them a dash of whisky in their milk. Aaagh!'

Jack, father of a toddler

'My mother-in-law babysat last week and told us when we got home that she left Sophie to cry to sleep because it was a temper tantrum – at seven weeks, mind you! I am still absolutely livid and don't really know what to do about this, except not to get her to babysit much any more.'

Lana, mother of an eight-week-old

Bring in the big guns

Finally, if you just haven't got the energy or confidence to defend yourself in the face of criticism or unwanted advice, it can help to bring in the big guns. Respond along the following lines: 'Our paediatrician/doctor/health nurse says we shouldn't let her cry – it'll weaken her muscles/raise her blood pressure/burn too many calories and affect her weight gain' or whatever else you can think up on the spur of the moment.

Chapter two
'Womb service'

Although hunger and pain rank high on the reasons-for-crying scale, adjusting to the world outside the womb is possibly one of the earliest (but one of the least explained) causes of newborns' crying.

'We read books about the hungry cry, tired cry, pooey nappy cry…the list goes on. Needless to say, these were of some help and when you tune into your little one (which is sometimes hard on zero hours sleep) you can hear the difference between their cries and interpret what their problem is. Some are easily fixed (i.e. nappy) but some are harder, especially once you have tried everything including driving around in the car at 2.30 a.m. (luckily the Ashes were on at the time in England, so I listened to the cricket). You surprise yourself about the lengths you will go to calm this little ball of stress and noise. You then stop the car after she goes to sleep and as soon as you turn it off she starts up crying again. Just keep the car running in the drive for a while. You need your sleep too.'

Pete, father of one

9 *Adjusting to the world outside the womb is possibly one of the earliest causes of newborns' crying. You can ease the transition from womb to world by creating a calm, welcoming environment which as far as possible resembles life in utero.*

Just for a moment, imagine yourself soaking in a warm bath by candlelight, listening to the sounds of hushed voices drifting from another room or soft music playing in the distance. Now imagine standing naked on a busy street corner in the middle of winter, with the headlights of a car shining in your face and loud traffic noise all around you. When you put yourself in your baby's bootees, it isn't difficult to understand the enormous physical and sensory changes from womb to room: in the watery world of the womb, your little one was naked, weightless and warm; he was comforted by the rhythm of your heartbeat and the rhythmic motion of his 'mother home'; and his need for food was automatically and immediately met. Leaving this dark, warm and soothing environment, a newborn must get used to new sensations: cold air moving across his skin and into his lungs, lights, direct sounds, smells, and surrounding stillness. Soon he will also learn the discomfort

of hunger and thirst, the sensations of feeding and digestion and the friction of clothing fibres against his sensitive
skin.

Is it any wonder that some babies express their confusion at these changes by crying? Babies who have a
difficult birth or are separated from their mother immediately after birth, especially if they are unwell or premature,
are more likely to communicate that they are 'missing the
womb', but this can happen even if your baby has a gentle birth experience. Although some babies will cry (and
cry) in spite of your best efforts, you can at least ease the
transition from womb to world by creating a calm, welcoming environment which, as far as possible, resembles
your baby's life in utero.

> 'We tried to put ourselves into her situation: she has come
> from a warm, comfortable, dark environment in mum's beau-
> tifully comfortable womb to this loud, bright, and constantly
> interrupting place we call our world. I would cry too, that's for
> sure. I cry and I have been out of my mother's womb for some
> 37 years now.
>
> 'I believe, if you think of them as you would yourself in cer-
> tain situations you will understand them better. Some days you
> don't want to be near anyone, other days you could take on

the world. Some days a person will just rub you up the wrong way and it takes all day to get over that incident. Babies act the same way, they just tell you their feelings by crying.'

Tony, father of a 14-month-old

'Cassidy was a healthy baby, 4110 grams and 55 centimetres long. After a gentle, unmedicated birth, his head popped out and he screamed, not just cried but screamed. Most babies murmur and make little noises before being totally roused. Not Cassidy. He opened his eyes and screamed. The only way to keep him quiet was on the breast. After a couple of hours of swapping sides every half an hour, we tried a bath. He fell asleep in the bath, but when I took him out, he woke instantly.

'He did have a nap that early evening, and when he woke at 9 p.m. I thought, "This is a nice time, half an hour for a feed, I'll be asleep by 10." Wrong. He continued swapping sides for a long time and then, at about 2 a.m. after I tried bathing him to get him to sleep, the midwives offered to take him so I could get some sleep. At 5 a.m. they bought him back because he wouldn't sleep.'

Merewyn, mother of one

'In hospital Daniel pierced the corridors with a blood-curdling scream the whole stay. Nurses ordered two neurological checks: all was fine and we all concluded he had a thumper of a headache after his traumatic birth.'

Fi, mother of one

'I had Evie in a birth centre where you only stay for 24 hours and then go home. No problems, I thought! The first week after we got home was probably the hardest week of my life. My partner and I were both inexperienced when it came to babies and had to learn quickly. The first night Evie cried pretty much all night no matter what we did. I spent my nights out in the lounge-room so Dan could get some sleep. He would usually get out of bed around 2 a.m. to find me rocking Evie and crying as much as she was! He would then take her and walk laps around the house until she eventually quietened down. I would use this time to get half an hour's sleep.

'This same thing happened every night for at least a week – each night I would think I could handle her crying, but I would always end up in tears and wait for Dan to come and rescue me.

'Evie eventually started to settle and cry less, and I began to feel more human. For a while, I was terrified of her crying while I was out (e.g. shopping) and was worried that people would judge me a bad mother or something. But if Evie cries in public now, I've learnt to not care what other people think!'

Cassie, mother of an eight-month-old

Introduce him to the world gradually

During the first six weeks of life, babies are especially sensitive. It is perfectly normal for a newborn to startle and cry at any abrupt change in stimulation, such as loud noises or sudden changes of position. They often keep their eyes tightly shut when in a brightly lit room or bright sunlight.

You can alleviate your baby's sensitivity by moving him slowly and smoothly to allow him to get used to changes in position, unwrapping him slowly to avoid exposing him to sudden temperature changes, talking to him gently, minimising handling by people outside the immediate family, and avoiding bright lights and loud noise. Although he will quickly get used to normal household hustle and bustle, places like shopping centres – with their intrusive lighting and clamour – can be overwhelming.

This doesn't mean you have to remain barefoot in the kitchen now you have a baby, just be aware how venturing out may affect both of you: plan short outings at first, and consider how the environment might affect your little one. Anticipate a bout of crying after a jaunt to stressful, noisy venues (including family gatherings), even if baby is quiet or sleeps most of the time you're out. At home, your newborn will probably be more alert and open his eyes to the world if you keep the lights reasonably dim at first. One suggestion is to bathe him in soft light by draping a veil of coloured silk over the cradle during the first few weeks; midwife Rahima Baldwin suggests a combination of blue and pink or rose-coloured silk. (Baby veils are available by mail order: see the Resources section.)

In other words, introduce your baby to the world gradually and respect his cues: if he starts to cry, looks unusually wide-eyed (startled), falls asleep when he would normally be awake, or otherwise seems distraught, take some time out together in a quiet place. Drape a blanket over your shoulder and your baby to block out excess visual stimuli, and offer him a breast/bottle/dummy as sucking is a calming, familiar activity (see 'Sucking for comfort' below).

> **10**   *Respect your baby's cues. If he starts to cry, looks unusually wide-eyed (startled!), falls asleep when he would normally be awake, or otherwise seems distraught, take some time out together in a quiet place.*

Sucking for comfort

Sucking is a comfort to babies and helps them relax. In fact, your baby quite possibly sucked his fingers even before he was born. In the early days especially, your baby will often

indicate that he wants the breast – nature's most convenient pacifier – by 'rooting' (turning his head towards the
breast and making grasping movements with his mouth)
even when he isn't hungry. Some mothers may find having a baby who wants to be almost constantly 'attached'
quite disconcerting, but be reassured, as he gets used to
the world and as his movements become more controlled
so he can easily find his fingers, your baby will not rely on
nursing so much as a form of comfort.

Offering a dummy may buy you some short-term relief
at times when your baby seems inconsolable, or it may
be helpful if he is a high-needs baby. However, there may
be some disadvantages that are worth serious consideration before you 'plug up' your baby, especially in the early
weeks (see 'Does your baby have a sucking problem?' on
page 74). Offering your young baby a clean finger to suck
if he isn't hungry will provide comfort without causing
'nipple confusion', since dummies encourage a 'thrusting'
tongue action, while a finger holds the baby's tongue flat in
a similar position to breastfeeding.

If you do find that a dummy helps to comfort your
baby, keep a supply of clean ones so that you always have
a replacement to hand if the one he's using gets lost or falls
on the ground mid-wail. Never attach a dummy to your

baby with a ribbon, as dangling ribbons are a strangling danger; *never* sweeten a dummy (or dip it in any other substance). Watch your baby's cues and if he spits the dummy out don't keep plugging him up again, as you run the risk of blocking his only means of communication – he may want his needs met in other ways, such as being fed, played with or talked to. Also remember that dummies can be more trouble than they prevent, as some babies who sleep with dummies are woken – and start crying – every time the dummy slips out of their mouth. For this reason, if you do use a dummy to help your baby relax, it's wise to remove it once he has fallen asleep.

> **11** If he spits the dummy out, don't keep plugging him up again, as you run the risk of blocking his only means of communication. He may want his needs met in other ways, such as being fed, played with or talked to.

Keep your baby close

Being separated from you will be stressful to your baby in the early days, when the only familiar things in his new world are the sound of your heartbeat and voice, and the comfort of your body close to his.

Based on observations of the animal world, many researchers claim that babies have an innate need for close physical contact with their parents. There are two types of infant-rearing amongst animals: caching and carrying. The 'caching' species are adapted to their mothers being absent for long periods: these animals do not cry, for this would attract predators, and their mothers' milk is extremely high in protein and fat to sustain the young for long periods. Humans are much closer to continuous-feeding, 'carrying' mammals such as anthropoid apes; our milk is identical to theirs in fat content, and our babies – like theirs – suckle slowly and cry (often loudly!) when they are distressed or out of contact with a parent's warm body.

Research shows that babies thrive on skin-to-skin contact, which provides warmth as well as the comforting scent of a loving parent. Holding your baby close will enhance bonding as well as neurological development: so relax and enjoy snuggles with your little one – you are not only helping him feel secure, but making him smarter as well! Hold him against your bare skin, nuzzle against his soft downy head, and inhale his delicious baby perfume.

12   *Holding your baby close will enhance bonding as well as neurological development: so relax and enjoy snuggles with your little one – you are not only helping him feel secure, but making him smarter as well!*

Baby-wearing

Carrying your baby in a sling gives you an extra pair of hands as you keep your baby close. As well, this constant contact helps you to become familiar with and respond to his pre-cry signals, which results in less frustration. Lower levels of stress hormones in your baby's bloodstream in turn result in a more relaxed, happy baby – and parent!

'With the arrival of my second baby, Chela, ten years after the first, I was much more relaxed as a mother and trusted my own intuition when it came to my baby's needs. She very clearly communicated that she did not like to be left alone (even if I was close by) and having her close against my body in a baby carrier just felt so right. She was happier, cried so much less, slept longer and deeper, and I had both my hands free to get on with my day. I feel baby-wearing not only strengthened my confidence as a mother, it deepened the bond between us and that is forever.'

Suzanne, mother of two

The familiar sound of a mother's voice has been shown to regulate an infant's early, unco-ordinated body movements, as the baby synchronises his movements with the rhythm of the mother's voice. When you carry your baby tummy-to-tummy and chest-to-chest against your body, your heartbeat, rhythmic movement and respiration have a balancing effect on your baby's irregular rhythms of waking, sleeping and digestion; it is also thought to help him regulate his developing nervous and hormonal systems, and promote day waking and night sleeping. Carrying your baby upright against your warm body will also help relieve symptoms of colic and reflux. And yes, your baby is safe sleeping in a sling.

Start carrying your baby in a sling as early as possible to get your own body used to his weight before he becomes too heavy. If you find baby-wearing a strain at first, use the sling for shorter periods and gradually increase the length of time as your muscles adapt. If your baby is very small, it may be wise to carry him horizontally, making sure the sling has adequate head support until he can hold his own head up. Most horizontal slings adapt to an upright position to accommodate babies as they grow.

Try on various slings (with a baby in them) before you buy one. Check for comfort: are the leg openings wide enough? Does the fabric chafe? Could a bigger baby climb or slip out? Will baby be supported if he falls asleep? Can he get his fingers caught? And for practicality: is the sling easily washable? Are the fasteners easy to do up properly? Most importantly, check that you can get the sling on easily without help.

13 *Carrying your baby upright against your warm body, as well as being a simple soother, will help relieve symptoms of colic and reflux.*

Swaddling

In his womb world, your baby's body was contained by the uterine wall. After birth, he not only has to get used to a new sense of open space but has to contend with his own primitive survival reflexes such as the 'startle reflex' which produces spontaneous, jerky movements even in sleep. This can be disturbing to babies, especially when their own flailing arm hits them in the face, and can be a cause of crying if baby startles himself awake. These reflexes will disappear as your baby's motor development allows voluntary, controlled movements to replace those erratic, uncontrolled ones (the startle reflex disappears at around three to four months, but it can last up to six months in some babies). But in the meantime you can provide a sense of security by 'swaddling' your little one – wrapping him firmly in a gauze or muslin sheet (in summer) or a cotton bunny rug or soft shawl (in cooler weather).

As baby grows, it is better developmentally if his movements aren't restricted. If your older baby will only sleep if he is wrapped, but is strong enough to get his arms out and disturb himself, or tends to become immobilised by his wrap when he rolls over, gradually wrap more and more loosely or wrap with one arm out, then the other, and then discard the wrap for sleeping – it is best to do this by the time he is around three or four months old. Some parents find it easy to transition from a wrap to a sleeping bag, which helps baby stay warm and secure without the worry of him being tangled in blankets. If you wrap him for feeds, leave his hands unwrapped so he can touch you – his tiny fingers have hundreds of nerve endings which receive and send messages to his developing brain.

There are various methods of swaddling a baby. Each time I have given birth, hospital staff have shown me a different way to wrap my cherub – and each one has shown me as though this was the only correct way. What I discovered for myself is that babies are individuals – right down to how firmly they like to be swaddled: some love to be wrapped tightly, while others like to 'hang loose'; some babies are happy to have their hands enclosed, while others seem to prefer them free so they can suck their fingers for comfort. Then, of course, there are babies who don't like to be wrapped at all.

One simple method of wrapping:

1   Lay the sheet with a corner facing up, forming a diamond.

2   Fold the top corner down towards the centre of the sheet, to form a longer straight edge across the top. Then, if your baby is awake, place him on the sheet and draw one side across his body, rolling him a little so you can tuck that edge under him. Tuck his arms in, or leave his hands out so that he can discover his fingers. If your baby has fallen asleep in your arms, gently hold him against your shoulder with one arm and wrap him while you are holding him – lying him flat while he is unwrapped may startle and wake him.

3   Fold the bottom point up over his feet and roll the remaining side of the sheet across his body. As you do this, you can tuck the point into the top of the sheet at your baby's neck if you are enclosing his hands, or lower down if you are leaving his hands free; or just fold it around behind. Tucking in the bottom point is optional, too: it depends how long the sheet is relative to your baby.

Some mothers find they can help their babies differentiate between day and night by swaddling them loosely during the day and more firmly at night.

14   *You can provide a sense of security by 'swaddling' your newborn – wrapping him firmly in a gauze or muslin sheet (in summer) or a cotton bunny rug or soft shawl (in cooler weather).*

Out of the birthday suit

Discomfort is a common cause of crying and irritability. Although we tend to take dressing babies for granted, this too is a new sensation for a newborn and clothing can irritate his delicate skin. Getting clothes on and off can upset some babies, and clothing can also make them uncomfortably hot or cold.

So when you choose clothing for your baby, consider comfort before style: larger, loose clothing is better than clothes that fit so snugly that they cause overheating or restrict baby's movements. Natural fabrics (pure cotton, wool or silk) are preferable to synthetics, which don't absorb perspiration and may irritate sensitive skins. Babies may, though, also find direct skin contact with wool irritating, so if you need wool for warmth do put a pure-cotton t-shirt underneath.

Some babies will cry as you pull clothing over their heads, so look for designs with envelope necks and front openings, and make sure there is easy nappy-changing access. Also check the workmanship, especially seams under arms and at the crotch: are they well-stitched and overlocked, or will they fray easily (loose threads can irritate and can catch around little body parts like fingers and toes)? Do zippers go up and down easily (these can pinch delicate skin)? Are buttons sewn on firmly (so they won't fall off and become choking hazards)?

How you wash your baby's clothing can also impact on his comfort: residues of laundry powder can irritate his skin, so use a gentle pure soap and rinse well.

> **15** *Turn jumpsuits inside-out before washing, and check for loose threads, hairs or pieces of fluff which could twist painfully around a tiny baby toe.*

Although bare feet are best for babies as they become mobile, if you use socks for warmth choose ones without patterns as these are less likely to have loose threads (to get an idea of this, turn a sock inside-out and see the number of threads inside a patterned sock and the absence of them in a plain one).

Unless they are unwell, babies are more likely to feel too cold than too hot. A general rule of thumb is to dress baby in one more layer of clothing than you would wear; if he seems sweaty or hot to touch (feel his chest), remove a layer.

A relaxation bath

A bath will often soothe a tense, crying baby. Take your baby back to the weightless, watery world of the womb with a relaxation bath (as opposed to a wash in the bath). Run a warm, deep bath in an adult tub: the water needs to be deep enough for your baby to float and should be as comfortably warm as you would have it yourself (check the temperature with your wrist before you put baby in). Although essential oils are not recommended for newborns, when your baby is over three months you may like to add these to the bath: as noted elsewhere, lavender and chamomile have calming properties. (Check with a natural-health practitioner about which oils and bath products are safe for babies.) Either use a ready-made baby bath mix such as Aromababy, or make your own: mix a drop of your chosen oil with 20 ml of full-cream milk before adding it to the water, to make sure that the oil is thoroughly dispersed – if not, even little drops can burn baby's delicate skin.

Support your baby in the water so he is floating on his tummy. If you feel a bit dubious about holding him this way, floating on his back will still be calming. If your baby is a newborn, he may settle more easily if he is contained as you bathe him: inside the womb your baby was confined and not floating all stretched out. By dimming the lights and bathing with your newborn by candlelight, you will help him recall the safety of his womb world and you will be able to hold him close and support him as he gradually relaxes and uncurls his limbs. Bathing together is especially helpful if bonding has been interrupted by early separation, or a difficult birth or feeding experience. It can also be lovely bonding time for father and baby.

Newborns can lose body heat very quickly after a bath and a cold baby will be more difficult to settle. Also, if you lay your baby flat to dry him, this can trigger his startle reflex and he may start to scream – which of course defeats the purpose of a relaxation bath. Rather than exposing your baby to cool air and risking more crying, wrap him in two warmed towels and cuddle him. The heat trapped in the towels will dry most of your baby's body as the warmth relaxes him. Then you can remove the damp towel next to his body and with the outer, dryer towel gently dry his crevices (neck, underarms, groin, between fingers and toes).

To bathe safely with your baby, it is best to have somebody else to help you get in and out of the bath. If you are on your own, place your baby on a towel that is spread over a baby seat or bouncinette next to the bath. When you are comfortably in the bath, reach over and lift baby in with you. When you need to get out, place baby back in his bouncer, wrap him in the towel to keep him warm while you get dried and pop on your dressing gown, then dress your baby and snuggle together – bliss!

If your baby is crying and refusing to feed, he may settle down and breastfeed in the bath if you feel like one too.

16   *A bath will often soothe a tense, crying baby. Take him back to the weightless, watery world of the womb with a deep, warm relaxation bath.*

Alternative therapies

Complementary therapies – a gentle treatment option – are becoming an increasingly popular resource for parents. Osteopathy and chiropractic care are claimed to alleviate distress from the birth process, particularly after difficult deliveries. And naturopathy, aromatherapy and homoeopathy are said to be effective in the treatment of colic. Always check that any therapist you are considering using is registered with the appropriate authority and is also experienced in working with babies.

'We have now had two sessions with the osteopath and don't need to go again until Jack starts to crawl. He can certainly move his head a lot more freely since his treatments and is happier, but it's hard to say whether this would have happened anyway and how many of his changes were developmental considering his appointments were six weeks apart. I guess I'll never know whether it was his twisted neck that contributed to all the crying in the first place or whether us finding it proved to be a coincidence, but our baby is much happier after treatment. I'm still happy that I took him to the osteopath and will certainly take any future children there if we have problems – if only to make me feel better!'

Rachel, mother of a five-month-old

'Sam had a difficult birth and, I believe, a really bad headache for at least the first week. I took him to a chiropractor for some cranial work when he was three weeks old and I saw a great *improvement, in crying and general distressed states. It was also helpful to settle colicky-type problems. We have seen the chiropractor regularly since then and it has helped with constipation too. The nicest part is that he giggles while being adjusted! We visit a practitioner in Maroubra and it takes me an hour to get to the appointment, but I value what it is doing to keep our baby on track.'*

Fi, mother of a nine-month-old

Chapter three
Is she hungry?

Especially in the early months, hunger is one of the first causes of crying to eliminate. In the first weeks, babies' tummies are only the size of their tiny fists and so simply don't hold enough food to go long between feeds, day or night. Babies regulate the volume and composition of your milk by their sucking and by how often they feed. This will vary as they grow (as their tummies grow and hold more, and as they become more active and expand more energy, they will require a larger quantity of milk), so although you may receive advice to schedule your baby's feeds, this is likely to cause unnecessary crying. It is best to learn your baby's hunger cues (squirming and making sucking noises, bringing his hand to his mouth, sucking on his fingers or 'rooting' at the breast) – crying is a late hunger signal for most babies.

> **17** In the first weeks, babies' tummies are only the size of their tiny fists and so simply don't hold enough food to go long between feeds, day or night.

If your baby has been a happy feeder but then suddenly refuses the breast or starts crying when you attempt to feed her, she could be teething or 'coming down with something' – such as a cold, an ear infection (in which case pressure within the ears increases when baby is in a horizontal position, and this will cause pain), or thrush (see 'Is it thrush?' on page 76). Alternatively, she may be expressing her sensitivity to your deodorant, perfume or soap (if you're breastfeeding, avoid using soap on your nipples: it will remove the natural protective oils that keep your nipples supple and help baby recognise your 'smell'). Or, if you have been trying to enforce a rigid feeding schedule, breast refusal may be your baby's way of telling you that this isn't appropriate.

18   *Learn to identify your baby's hunger signals (squirming, grunting and 'rooting' at the breast), to avoid hunger cries – crying is a late hunger signal for most babies.*

If you have eliminated these as possible causes, it may be a matter of re-establishing your happy breastfeeding relationship. Start by feeding in a quiet space with dim lighting, to avoid distractions. It may also be easier to encourage your baby to feed while she is dozing and you are relaxed:

for night feeds, consider taking her into bed with you to maintain closeness.

Is supply meeting demand?

If you have a crying baby, you are almost certain to hear comments such as, 'Are you sure you have enough milk?' or 'Maybe your milk isn't strong enough.' (By the way, this last proposition is *never* true, although in our mothers' day it was a common belief.) It is much more likely that she is simply hungry: it is perfectly normal for a breastfed baby to need feeding every two hours at first – and that means two hours from the *beginning* of one feed to the beginning of the next, not two hours between feeds – which is about how long it takes breast milk to be digested. It is also common for babies to need a 'cluster' of feeds close together in the evening

If your baby is solely breastfed, you can be confident that she is getting enough milk if she is steadily gaining weight and is having at least six to eight pale (dark urine is a sign of dehydration), wet cloth nappies (or at least five full/heavy disposable ones) every day. Even if your baby gains weight slowly, consider whether this could be a family trait – you can't expect to get rats from mice! It can also be reassuring to refer to the World Health Organization's baby weight charts, as these have been compiled with breastfed babies as the norm. The older charts used by some health organisations are based on predominantly formula-fed infants, who have a different growth pattern.

'After an initial good weight gain, our third baby became an often-crying baby. Her infant welfare book recorded 'poor weight gain'. At each visit, I endured a humiliating interrogation about everything from my nutritional status to my marital happiness. My family threw around comments like, "Got her on a bad quarter?"

'Luckily, our two older boys had been strapping big babies themselves, and, in spite of her low weight gains my baby was bright, alert and active (she crawled at five months) and even though "well-wishers" warned me that if she didn't grow her brain wouldn't grow and she would be "retarded", her head circumference developed at a normal rate (indicating brain growth – she was dux of her school and is now at university). I reassured myself that I was the same mother with the same breasts, perhaps there was another reason for the crying. Meanwhile, I clung to the desert island theory. Picture yourself on a desert island: no clocks, no "experts", no scales and no

"helpful" advice from anybody. Whenever your baby cries or fusses, you offer the breast and ask questions later. You nurse until your baby seems satisfied.

'As if to prove hunger was not the reason for her crying spells, our dainty daughter utterly refused to eat solids until she was eleven months old (that, of course, raised even more unwanted advice). Now a young adult, our daughter is still petite – just like her mother!'

Gabby, mother of four

'Around three months, Zac's weight gains slowed. I was advised to complementary feed him. Of course other friends and relatives were not backward in suggesting that I "don't put myself through it", that if I put him on the bottle he'd gain weight and start to sleep. The first night I made up a bottle of formula and fed it to him at 11 p.m. when he woke (he guzzled it down), and settled down for my full night's sleep – two hours later I was feeding him another bottle of formula…two hours later, another bottle… The theory that I'd get more sleep wasn't working. I was getting up to warm bottles when I could have just rolled over and fed him. I quickly abandoned that plan.'

Barb, mother of three

Is she having a growth spurt?

It is also important to remember that a growth spurt – commonly claimed to occur at six weeks and at three months, but possible at any time – can give your baby an increased appetite, which may cause grizzling if she is not satisfied whether she is breast- or bottle fed. Most babies *double* their birth weight by the time they are five to six months old, and *triple* it in a year. If your baby is having a growth spurt her hunger cries don't mean you are running out of milk but rather that she will need to suck more often for a few days to give your breasts the message that they need to produce more milk. If you offer a 'top-up' bottle, your baby won't need to empty your breasts and they won't get the message to increase milk production.

Is she hungry, or just thirsty?

Whether she is crying because she is hungry or simply thirsty, your baby will be able to regulate the type of milk she takes in if you allow her to set the pace. The composition of breast milk changes during a feed: the first (fore) milk, which is rather like skim milk, is thirst-quenching, which is why a baby will often have very short, frequent feeds on hot days. As the feeding progresses, the fat content increases and more closely resembles whole milk. Her hunger will be satisfied by longer sucking periods when she gets to the fatty hind milk which is passed into your ducts by the 'let-down' reflex. Your baby needs to 'finish' the first breast first in order to get the hind milk, but if she is satisfied with only one side you may need to express a little milk for your own comfort and as a preventative measure against mastitis. One solution is to feed baby on one side until she chooses to drop off, burp her and/or have a little play and a nappy change, then give her the other side before you put her back to bed. This way she will seem to go longer before crying for another feed, too.

19 *A growth spurt – common at six weeks and at three months, but possible at any time – can give your baby an increased appetite, which may cause grizzling if she is not satisfied.*

Watch your baby, not the clock

Trying to impose a strict feeding schedule rather than watching your baby's cues to be fed is likely to result in more crying and may even be a health risk. When you compare a baby's needs to those of an adult (who is generally trying *not* to gain weight – at least not to double or triple their current size!), it is easy to understand that imposing a strict regime which restricts the duration and amount of your baby's feeds is not only unrealistic and unkind but also liable to hinder her blooming. Consider how often you eat, drink, nibble, snack or sip through an average day? Did you know that you would be having a cup of coffee at four o'clock this afternoon, or did you just feel like one? Did you tell your work colleagues you couldn't have lunch with them at midday because you weren't scheduled to eat till one o'clock? Doesn't your hunger and thirst change according to the weather and your own activity level?

There is also evidence that allowing babies to feed according to their own appetite, rather than imposing feeding schedules, is more compatible with the biology of mothers and babies. Although breastfeeding according to a schedule may seem to work at first, many women who use strict feeding schedules in the early weeks find that their milk supply dwindles and their baby may be weaned by about three months. By restricting feeds or repeatedly spacing them out with dummies, you may limit the development of the hormonal process that enhances ongoing milk production. Early and frequent breastfeeding will promote a continuing milk supply, which means that your baby will get lots of milk and be less likely to cry with hunger.

Another reason for watching your baby, rather than the clock, is that mothers have varying breast milk storage capacities. Ultrasound studies by biochemist Dr Peter Hartmann at the University of Western Australia have shown that milk storage capacity can vary up to three times as much between individual women (this is not necessarily related to breast size and doesn't influence milk production ability). This means that while some women who have a large milk storage capacity will be able to feed their babies enough milk to go three or four hours between feeds (providing their baby has a big enough stomach), other women will need to feed their babies more often. For women with a smaller milk storage capacity, a three- or four-hourly feeding schedule could result in a hungry, unsettled baby and a mother who questions her ability to produce enough milk. Instead of becoming stressed about how much milk your breasts are making, think in terms of drinking out of a cup – you can still drink a litre of water whether you drink it from a large cup or several small cupfuls. If you allow your baby to nurse whenever he lets you know he is hungry, you will never have to worry about your milk storage capacity.

Milk production and infant intake are also influenced by the fat content of your milk and the degree of breast emptying at any given feeding. According to Dr Hartmann's research, an empty breast will make milk more quickly, while a full breast will make milk more slowly. This means that milk production will speed up or slow down according to how hungry your baby is and how well he empties your breasts. If he sucks vigorously and 'empties' the breast (because you make milk continuously, your breasts will never be completely empty), production will speed up. If he doesn't take much milk from the breast when feeding, your breasts will get the message to make less milk.

If you follow your baby's lead, your milk supply will catch up with your baby's increased demand whether it is due to a growth spurt or to other factors such as an impending illness, and she will quickly stop crying and settle down into a more predictable rhythm again. Take it easy for a few days and offer your baby lots of skin-to-skin contact as this will help stimulate your milk production hormones. Sit back with baby on your bare chest and watch a DVD or take baby and a good book to bed with you (if this isn't baby No. 1, see 'Sibling harmony' on page 255 for tips on keeping your older child amused while you do so), and remember that the more your baby sucks the more milk you will make.

Do you need a herbal boost?

Liquid in equals liquid out, so all that yummy mummy's milk needs to be replaced! If you are breastfeeding, you not only need to heed your baby's hunger cries to maintain your milk supply, you also need to listen to your own body signals of hunger (see 'Eat to boost your energy' on page 261) and thirst. Having a drink while you breastfeed will help keep you flowing. Plain water is just fine, and extra fluids can include juice, soups and milk drinks, although it isn't necessary to 'drink milk to make milk'. Some mothers use herbal remedies such as raspberry-leaf or fenugreek tea, or fenugreek or blessed thistle tablets (not milk thistle) to help boost their milk supply.

For centuries, raspberry-leaf tea has been considered the 'herb supreme' among pregnant women. High in nutrients including calcium, iron and B vitamins, as well as chemicals that produce a direct effect on the pregnant uterus, it is claimed to make childbirth easier. Many women continue to drink the tea after childbirth as it is thought to restore the reproductive system, help nourish the new mother and enhance breast milk production.

Fenugreek, one of the oldest medicinal herbs, was highly regarded by Hippocrates and other Greek and Roman physicians. It is high in nutrients such as protein, vitamin C, niacin and potassium, and is taken by Egyptian women to relieve menstrual pain (in China it is used to treat male impotence!) Fenugreek has been shown to be a potent stimulator of breast-milk production – its use was associated with increases in milk production of as much as 900 per cent in an Egyptian study. Fenugreek tea, or 2–3 fenugreek tablets three times a day (some brands rec-ommend a lower dosage, but this may not be effective for increasing milk production) will usually increase milk sup-ply within 24 hours. In fact, some mothers say this stuff has such potent effects that it might be sensible to start low and gradually increase the dosage as necessary, to avoid engorgement. A good guide is to take fenugreek until your perspiration smells a little 'sweet': this doesn't appear to have any negative effects on the taste of your milk – at least not according to baby reactions!

It is probably not necessary to continue taking these herbal remedies once they have done the trick, as long as you comply with the law of supply and demand (as above), eat a nutritious and varied diet, and drink adequate fluids. And a word of caution: these teas are for *you*, not your baby. It is not advisable to give herbal remedies to your baby, because they may contain potent active ingredients – including sugar and caffeine – that could be harmful to babies. Read labels carefully and avoid teas with caffeine yourself, if you are breastfeeding and a calm baby is your objective!

> **20** *Some mothers use herbal remedies such as raspberry-leaf or fenugreek tea, or fenugreek or blessed thistle tablets (not milk thistle) to help boost their milk supply.*

Do you need a health check?

If you are worried about a low milk supply in spite of trying all the basic tips to remedy this, it would be sensible to have your haemoglobin (iron levels are often low after childbirth) and thyroid function checked.

As well as extreme tiredness, common symptoms of low thyroid function can include swelling of the thyroid gland (in the front of your neck), dry skin, depression, and intolerance to cold. If a blood test shows that you have an underactive thyroid, there are medications that work fairly quickly and can be safely used while you are breastfeeding. Smoking can also reduce your milk supply, and will certainly affect your baby's health (see 'Fags, booze and other vices' on page 115).

'At five weeks Jeremy had not even recovered his birthweight and the health visitor and my GP urged me to supplement him with formula, which I was very reluctant to do. A couple of well-meaning friends told me that Jeremy looked as if he was starving, and I felt embarrassed to show him off in public he looked so unwell. I dreaded the weighing sessions which occurred every few days and I felt each time as if I was on trial. I felt I had failed, and I was totally confused as to why when I had successfully breastfed two very large babies with no problems at all, I could not sustain little Jeremy who was at birth some two pounds lighter than his siblings. At the same time breast-feeding counsellors recommended I try to increase my milk supply by expressing milk so I hired a breast pump. Needless to say, I had very little time in which to try to do this. I also failed to see what was really happening. I was exhausted from looking after my four-year-old and my two-year-old. I had very little sleep with Jeremy's constant crying. A vicious circle resulted. I was too tired to make enough milk, he got more and more hungry and unsettled, therefore I got more tired, and so on.'

Anne, mother of three

Surround yourself with positive voices

Tension and anxiety can inhibit the let-down reflex and affects your milk flow. If your baby is grizzling, well-meant advice is likely to start flowing faster than your milk, which will probably compound the problem. At such times, it is normal to worry that you might be losing your milk.

If you find tension is affecting your milk flow, practise relaxation breathing and visualise milk flowing over a waterfall as you begin breastfeeding. Also, try to give your baby the impression that you are relaxed, even if you aren't: let your shoulders drop and relax your arms so she doesn't sense your tension, and handle her with slow movements – fast, jerky actions will convey your anxiety and upset your baby, which may in turn cause her to arch her back and struggle against the breast.

'My mother, who thinks that breasts were put on a woman's chest to attract the opposite sex, insists that there is something evil and unholy about breast milk – it is, after all, a bodily fluid. She maintained that I obviously could not breastfeed and so I should instantly put my daughter on "the tinned stuff" – it comes from a tin, after all, and is obviously not a bodily fluid. She had no faith in my body to produce milk and told me stories about mothers who starved their babies to death.'

Mary, mother of a ten-month-old

'We had experienced a wonderful birth at home – everything we could have imagined and more. For the first two days all he did was eat and sleep, he was so peaceful. By the morning of Day 3, my milk had still not come in and I was starting to get anxious. I had managed to keep visitors away from the house until now in my attempt to maintain the intimacy of the birth, and yet even the few who came seemed too many. As I tried furiously and very clumsily to learn to breastfeed my baby, the comments ranged from, "What's so hard: you just bang him on your boob," to "Hasn't that baby eaten yet?"

'I went from feeling incredibly empowered by the amazing birth to suddenly feeling ashamed and embarrassed because I didn't know "instinctively" how to breastfeed my baby successfully. My stress levels started to rise enormously and as a result, my baby started to cry. I firmly believe in retrospect that it was this feeling of outside pressure that contributed to Finn developing colic. He seemed to be fine all morning with just Dan and me for company, but as soon it came time for visitors I would tense up in anticipation of more "judgement" and he would start to squirm and become irritated. By the time the visitors got there, he always seemed to be out of control. I can see now that it was actually me that was secretly out of control and he was just crying the tears I refused to shed.'

Melinda, mother of one

21 *Try to give your baby the impression that you are relaxed, even if you aren't: let your shoulders drop and relax your arms so she doesn't sense your tension, and handle her with slow movements.*

Meanwhile it is important to surround yourself with positive voices: people who will reassure you that you *are* doing a great job and that you *do* have enough milk for your baby, rather than advising you to hit the bottle. Although it is never too late to seek support, the best time to enlist your cheering squad is *before* you actually have a screaming baby in your arms (day and night!) Your partner should be your No. 1 cheerleader. Yes, Dad, you: your role is to protect your beloved and your child from anybody (even your own mother) who so much as whispers, 'Perhaps she needs a bottle' (see also 'A little advice goes a long way' on page 28).

If you don't have friends or relatives who fit the 'positive voice' job spec., attend a support group (see Resources section) such as the Australian Breastfeeding Association or the La Leche League. You will get to know people who can help you if you have difficulties (it is always easier to call somebody you know and trust rather than a complete stranger). Don't ever underestimate what a difference a calm voice on the end of a telephone can make to an inconsolable baby (and mother!)

> **22**   *Surround yourself with positive voices: people who will reassure you that you are doing a great job and that you do have enough milk for your baby, rather than advising you to hit the bottle.*

Is breastfeeding difficulty causing the crying?

Sometimes your baby's blues (and your own) are due to breastfeeding problems, rather than a low milk supply. If your baby (and you) are finding breastfeeding difficult, take heart: most problems are quite easily remedied once they are identified. Please don't hesitate to seek help if you and your baby are struggling to master the art of breastfeeding. In the meantime, here are some common reasons for babies crying instead of feeding.

Does your baby have a sucking problem?
Sometimes babies have difficulty sucking effectively. If this is the case with your baby, it is a good idea to consult a health professional. A lactation consultant (many midwives

or infant health nurses are certified lactation consultants) can check that your baby is correctly positioned at the breast and show you how to help her suck effectively, or refer you to appropriate help. Sucking difficulties may also be an indicator of conditions or disorders which require medical attention. These are best diagnosed and treated as early as possible.

If you are breastfeeding, it is preferable not to give your baby bottles or a dummy in the first four to six weeks, as this can cause 'nipple confusion': the different sucking action required may make baby less effective at emptying your breasts and so cause your milk supply to dwindle. A recent American study showed that dummy use may be an *indicator* – rather than a cause – of breastfeeding difficulties. There is also a risk that using a dummy will interfere with your baby's signals that she is hungry and it can be all too easy to unintentionally allow a dummy to become a mother substitute as you let your baby suck a bit longer so you can finish just one more task. If it is inconvenient to offer the breast (although flashing a nursing bra will almost certainly guarantee you prompt service at the bank!), offering your baby a clean finger to suck may avert a full-volume yell until you can breastfeed or use other tactics to settle her.

23 *If it is inconvenient to offer the breast (although flashing a nursing bra will almost certainly guarantee you prompt service at the bank!), offering your baby a clean finger to suck may avert a full-volume yell.*

Is it thrush?

If your baby suddenly seems to have trouble latching on or fusses unusually while breastfeeding, and feeding seems painful (for *both* of you) thrush (*Candida albicans*, a yeast infection) is a possible cause. It commonly occurs if mother or baby have been on antibiotics (which kill the natural gut bacteria), during summer and in hot humid climates (which encourage yeast growth).

Look inside her mouth: thrush produces a white cheesy substance, which won't wipe away, on the insides of your baby's cheeks or on her tongue. In the early stages, thrush may not be obvious in your baby's mouth – if you are breast-feeding, your first warning may be excruciating, shiny red nipples and she may develop a sore, angry-looking nappy rash. A doctor will prescribe antifungal cream and medication. To prevent reinfection, apply an antifungal cream to your nipples, wash your bras frequently, use disposable nursing pads and boil all dummies, teats and toys that come into contact with baby's mouth. Insist that everybody who handles your baby washes their hands first.

If thrush is persistent, eliminate refined sugar and alcohol from your diet, increase your intake of plain yogurt containing live cultures, or take acidophilus tablets (the potent ones are kept in the refrigerator at the chemist or health-food shops) to increase the 'good' bacteria that control yeast in your gut.

24 *If your baby suddenly seems to have trouble latching on or fusses unusually while breastfeeding, and feeding seems painful (for* both *of you) thrush (*Candida albicans, *a yeast infection) is a possible cause.*

Don't rush her off milk

It is quite likely that you'll be told that your baby is crying because she is hungry and that filling her up with some solid food will 'calm' her or even make her sleep longer. Similarly you may be advised to wean her. There are, however, no advantages in either course: milk satisfies all a baby's nutritional needs till around the middle of the first year and breast milk contains organisms and proteins that offer protection against bacteria and viruses.

Changing to solids is not a solution

Introducing solids early is unlikely to comfort an unsettled baby and in fact could compromise her health: until around six months a baby's kidneys cannot cope with the increased load that solid food places on them, and her immune system is less able to tolerate antigens in foods that may cause allergies. And remember that adverse reactions to new foods, such as rashes and tummy aches, will cause more crying!

It is best to watch your baby's signals that she is ready for solid foods. As well as an increase in appetite and an interest in family foods (she grabs the food you are eating as it passes within reach!), a baby who is ready for solids will have good head and neck control; she will have lost the rooting reflex; she no longer pushes her tongue out when she opens her mouth to eat; and she now uses the swallowing reflex, moving her tongue from the front of her mouth to the back to swallow.

25   *Introducing solids early is unlikely to comfort an unsettled baby and in fact could compromise her health.*

Weaning might make it worse

If you have a crying baby and are breastfeeding, it may well be suggested that you wean her. Even if this comes from a health professional it is worth getting a second opinion, since weaning may cause a whole new range of difficulties, including preventable health problems and distress for both you and your baby.

> 'It dawned on me slowly that there was something wrong with my baby, William. At the time, I was dealing with his older brother, whom I believed was a very demanding toddler, not yet verbal, and possibly developmentally delayed. As we struggled through the early screening and diagnosis of our older son, I know now that I failed to notice the signs that his younger brother would also face great challenges in life. He often had a vacant gaze, lack of interest in toys and people, and bouts of sudden, unexplained crying.
>
> 'Over the months, approaching his first birthday, William's older brother entered an early intervention program and began what would become a life project for our family. Special education teachers, individual education plans, speech therapy, occupational therapy, medical specialists all played a role. Meanwhile, William picked up a few words, but soon lost them. He refused eye contact, failed to interact with people and pets,

showed little toddler curiosity, and was an angry, sad child in his own world. He became increasingly difficult to manage, throwing tantrums. For a year this continued, through early intervention, psychiatrists, paediatricians, and other specialists. During the whole time, the only comfort and means of communication we shared was through breastfeeding. It was our way to "talk", share, calm and comfort each other in a world that most of the time seemed to be spinning out of control.

'Finally, when he was three, a diagnosis came. Autism. Included in the original "to do list now that you have a diagnosis" from the doctor: contact early intervention services; see the social worker; start a variety of medications; get an EKG; and wean William from the breast.

'Everything seemed to have a reason, except for weaning. Why would I forcibly wean William, who showed no signs of wanting to stop feeding, when it was the only means of communication, expression of love, and quiet time we shared? The doctors couldn't offer an explanation, only that they felt it was worth "trying". They failed to acknowledge how important this one small piece of normal mothering was to me. Vulnerable and grieving, it took me a while to get my feet back under me. When I did, I took the coward's way out. When asked, I told them, "We're in the process of weaning", which technically we were, since William had been eating solids for a year or so.

'Over time, we adjusted to the diagnosis, but I never weaned William. On his fourth birthday, William gently patted my breast and said, "All done," and he was. He had decided it was time to wean. He never went back to the breast, but he still loves to put his head there and have a cuddle. I knew it then, but I believe it even more firmly now. Children know when it's time to wean. Listen to them, and you will know too.

'It's been nearly five years since William weaned himself. Of course he still has autism, and life is far from easy, but he is an affectionate and happy little boy. I believe that his life, and mine, would have been far more difficult had I forced him to wean before he was ready.'

Barbara, mother of two

26 *Weaning may cause a whole new range of difficulties, including preventable health problems and distress for both you and your and baby.*

The immunological benefits of breastfeeding last as long as your baby is breastfed. As baby grows, the composition of your breast milk changes to meet her changing needs. Some immune compounds in breast milk have been shown to increase at around six months (just when babies become mobile and are exposed to a greater range of germs) and also as she gets older and is breastfed less. On the other hand, bottle-fed babies experience more respiratory, ear and urinary tract infections, diarrhoea and allergies than their breastfed peers. This, of course, means more pain and discomfort – and, no doubt, more crying. So it makes sense to be as informed as possible about the mechanics of breastfeeding, so you can turn a deaf ear to comments that undermine your confidence.

Bottled-up?

If you are bottle-feeding and have a crying baby, you may feel even more stressed – as if the two are somehow related. This is not the case: just as breastfeeding is no guarantee of good mothering, bottle-feeding doesn't rule out a close relationship with your baby. If you are bottle-feeding, offer lots of skin contact and change baby's position from one side to the other during feeds, just as you would swap sides if you were breastfeeding, to ensure adequate stimulation to *both* sides of the infant (this affects eye and brain development as well as 'handedness'). For more information on bottle feeding, see page 114.

'There is no one to talk to about breastfeeding failure. I tried everywhere. I rang the hospital counselling service, but they couldn't, wouldn't, help. I even rang Sheila Kitzinger's birth crisis line. And you do feel like a failure. I was thrilled as a teen, watching my body bloom, and breasts come to their final stage of development when pregnant and breastfeeding. It's like having a disability, or a disease, like having to be on dialysis because your kidneys don't work. Your breasts aren't doing what they were made to do. What they must do.'

Lara, mother of one

Chapter four
Little pains

There is probably no more helpless feeling for a parent than knowing your baby is hurting, yet he doesn't have any way of telling you – apart from crying (or sometimes piercing screams) – exactly why he is hurting or what will make him feel better. Fortunately, lusty wails tend not to point to serious health problems – in fact, it is of more concern if a baby is unusually quiet or whimpering, or pale and quiet between cries, rather than yelling. Even cries that threaten to bring the house down often indicate a relatively straightforward ailment such as teething or a tummy ache, which are part and parcel of infant development.

Of course, sometimes a baby's pain *is* a symptom of illness – some tummy pains, in particular, require urgent medical care – so any time you have real concerns that your baby may be unwell it is wise to have him checked by an appropriate health professional. Usually if your baby is ill, he will have other symptoms such as a temperature, a rash, diarrhoea or vomiting, or a distended belly. Or he may refuse feeds, or wake screaming when you can rule out hunger as a cause. If your baby has a serious condition such as a bowel obstruction (these can be partial or complete, so he may still pass some bowel motions), his pain may come and go.

One illness that may not present with symptoms other than crying is a urinary tract infection: this does not come on as quickly as, for example, an ear infection and so may be present for several weeks before it is detected. If you have a persistently crying baby, it's worth asking your doctor to do a urine test to eliminate the possibility of an infection.

> **27** *Fortunately, lusty wails tend not to point to serious health problems – in fact, it is of more concern if a baby is unusually quiet or whimpering, or pale and quiet between cries, rather than yelling.*

When you need a doctor

You have a range of care options if your baby or child is unwell: from your local GP, who knows you and your child and will have your family's records at his fingertips, to large medical clinics that are usually open for longer

hours (babies don't always conveniently become ill during normal office hours), or a hospital emergency/casualty
department. As a parent, it is wise to know where all these
facilities are in relation to your home, and what costs are
involved. If, for instance, the nearest casualty department
is part of a private hospital, do you have to pay on the spot
or can you take the bill away with you and pay it later? Are
you eligible for a Medicare rebate, or can you claim the
costs on health insurance?

Help your doctor make a diagnosis

So you can describe your baby's symptoms accurately, it can
help to jot down some notes before you phone the clinic or
emergency department: you can bet your boots your mind
will have gone blank if you have to wait for a return phone
call while you're walking the floor with a crying baby. You
may need to convince a receptionist that your baby really
is unwell and you need an appointment *today*!

It will help if you describe what is happening, other
than crying. What is your baby's temperature? How long
has he had a fever? Is he lethargic? Cranky? Screaming?
Whimpering? Is he unable to sleep? When did he last feed?
How much is he drinking? Has he tried any new foods
recently? Does he have a rash? Is his skin pale, flushed or

mottled? What colour is his urine? Is he pulling at his ear? Is his ear red? Has he been vomiting? How many times has he vomited? Is there any blood in his vomit? When was his last bowel movement? What colour was it? Was it hard, runny or frothy, or did it contain mucus or blood?

28 *To describe your baby's symptoms accurately, it can help to jot down some notes before you phone the clinic or emergency department.*

Ask lots of questions

Don't be afraid or embarrassed to ask the doctor lots of questions – it's better to do so while you have his or her attention, rather than ringing back once you're at home again. For instance, if a medicine is prescribed, what is it and does it have any side-effects? How long are your baby's symptoms likely to last? Should you keep him at home? And so on.

Tummy troubles

Once, whenever a baby wailed with a 'tummy ache' it was attributed to gas or wind, so mothers diligently burped babies after feeds to bring up any swallowed air in order to prevent 'colic'. The theory was that swallowed air would later cause pain as it became trapped in the intestine. Although many parents and health practitioners have assumed that colic involves abdominal pain because the baby draws up his legs as he cries, some specialists claim that babies can't localise pain – that is, no matter where the pain originates, babies feel it in their tummies – while others suggest that the pain is a *result* of the crying (as the baby takes in gulps of air) rather than the cause.

Other experts, such as Sheila Kitzinger, acknowledge that feeding and digestion are remarkable sensations to a baby: 'The process of feeding and digestion is a momentous event for a baby. It can be disturbing and frightening. Intense sensations are produced: gnawing hunger, painful emptiness, passionate longing, rage, possession and triumph, and internal physiological states of pressure, fullness, spilling over, stretching, opening, together with intestinal contractions and rectal distension. All this can be an overwhelming experience, which we often over-simplify by describing it in terms of pain: "He's got a tummy-ache", "She's a colicky baby."'

Although massage is not a quick fix and is best used when baby is calm, there are specific massage techniques which may relieve tummy pain by moving gas (see 'Massage to tame tummy troubles' on page 229). You should not, however, use abdominal massage until baby's umbilical cord has dropped off (usually a week after birth) or if he seems to become more distressed when you massage him.

> **29** *Although massage is not a quick fix and is best used when baby is calm, specific massage techniques may relieve tummy pain by moving gas.*

Is it wind?

Nowadays there are other recognised causes of tummy pains than wind, and I talk about these in the following pages. However, as adults we are familiar with the sharp ache between our shoulderblades caused by trapped wind, usually after we have indulged in rich or acidic foods (obviously not the reason why babies might need to burp). Sometimes babies may feel uncomfortable too if they have a trapped air bubble. Although there are cultures who never burp their babies, it is still fairly common practice in our culture to do this after a feed – perhaps people who don't burp babies tend to carry their infants upright in slings, so any trapped wind is brought up naturally.

To burp your baby, simply sit him on your lap, with one hand against his tummy and the finger and thumb of this hand supporting his chin. Tilt his upper body slightly forward and gently rub his back with the palm of your other hand. Alternatively, you can hold him upright against your shoulder and gently pat his back (drape a nappy or towel over your shoulder to catch any milky spills!) There is no need to thump your baby vigorously, or to worry if he doesn't 'burp'.

Is it 'colic'?

Your baby was just fine only a few minutes ago. Now he is screaming inconsolably, drawing his legs up and perhaps clenching his fists. He is bright red in the face and he looks furious about the pain he is obviously experiencing. Yet he is otherwise healthy. 'Colic', nod your advisers.

The term colic, derived from a Greek word *kolikos* (meaning 'colon'), was long defined by many health professionals as an acute, sharp pain in the abdomen. It was generally thought to be caused by digestive problems such as a build-up of gas in the stomach. Experts now tend to define colic as a pattern of loud, persistent screaming, rather than an ailment, and it is now attributed to other causes besides tummy pain.

Colic is scary, especially for first-time parents. The crying spells most commonly occur in the evening, when mothers' and babies' reserves are lowest. The mother's levels of the 'coping' hormones prolactin and cortisol are lowest around 6 p.m. Levels of fat and protein in breast milk are also lower toward evening, and in the early months a baby's own biological rhythms may be disturbed by fluctuations in temperature, hormonal concentration and sleep patterns.

It's not your fault!

Colic has been described as a 'rule of three': unexplained crying that occurs during the first three months of life, lasts longer than three hours a day, happens on more than three days in any one week, and persists for at least three weeks. It typically starts at about two weeks and can last four to six months, but its onset, severity and duration vary widely – just like babies do.

The most commonly cited possible causes of colic are immaturity of the nervous system, immaturity of the digestive system, and infant temperament. It seems that 'colicky' babies may be less able to tune out stimulation or move smoothly from one state of consciousness (such as sleeping or being alert) to another, remaining stuck in this crying state. The trouble is that parents – especially first-time ones – often feel inadequate and blame themselves for their baby's colic. But take heart, it's neither your inexperience nor your nervousness causing your child's pain – your tension is a perfectly normal response to your infant's distress, not the cause of it. You are likely to feel even more tense if you lack support, and particularly if you are criticised for 'giving in' to your crying, colicky baby. Remember: he is not 'manipulating' you, he is not a 'difficult' child, and you are not 'spoiling' him by trying to give him comfort.

'I can honestly say that the hardest part for me about having a newborn baby was the crying that came with colic. It was something I had never given any thought to until he was born and then when it started it felt like it would never stop. What made it worse was that no one seemed to notice it in the way that I did. No matter whether he was whimpering or full-blown screaming, it all felt the same: it tore at my very insides – sometimes I felt that it had penetrated my soul.

'It got to a point where I became so overwhelmed with the sound of him that even in my dreams I was haunted by

the sound of crying babies. It felt as if his cry was stripping my nerves of all patience and stamina, and that eventually I would snap. I will admit openly that the thought of hurting him definitely crossed my mind more than once. I was fine for the first few hours, but once it became dark and I wanted to sleep myself I started to resent the fact that this little creature was keeping me awake, for no better reason than to scream the walls down. I was happy to feed him on demand, to massage him, get in a deep bath with him, rock him to sleep, but when none of these things worked and I was still holding an inconsolable baby, the thought of throwing him against the wall suddenly didn't seem so deranged. Luckily I had a wonderfully supportive partner who was always happy to take over where I left off – so I never did get to breaking point.

'I can now really understand how easily some parents find themselves hurting their babies – you can have the best intentions and heaps of patience and yet eventually it all just breaks down under the pressure of constant screaming.'

Joanne, mother of one

What can you do about it?

Whatever the cause, having a 'colicky' baby is invariably distressing – in fact, families in this situation are usually in crisis mode, which can create a vicious circle as their stress feeds back to the baby. Colic can also have negative effects on your relationship with your baby.

'My now nine-month-old daughter, Annalise, suffered from colic as a newborn which meant hours of crying (both of us) and lots of "experts" offering advice. We tried the advice that sounded worthwhile and politely forgot the rest as soon as we were told. After about three months she started to overcome this painful thing and life started to settle down. We consulted a naturopath about the colic and she was able to assist. However, what seemed to work the best was small, frequent breastfeeds and lots of cuddles, mum and dad included.'

Kristy, mother of one

'Having had two colicky babies, I was prepared for a third. I was thus pleasantly surprised that Jeremy slept really well for the first few days of his life. He also took well to breastfeeding initially.

'After the first week things began to go downhill. Jeremy was not latching on the breast well, not wanting to feed and crying more and more. It seemed that the more I fed him the worse the colic became, so I began to time the feedings and I left at least two hours between feeds. At its worst I was surviving on as little as two to three hours sleep at night. Jeremy also

failed to develop normal yellow breastfed-baby stools. I did not take this as seriously as I should as my baby book said it could take as long as three weeks for the green stools to disappear.

'At five weeks, we were referred to the hospital where, to my surprise and relief, we were given a great deal of support and help. The paediatrician advised me to eliminate cows milk and cows-milk products from my diet. Jeremy also had bad reflux (regurgitation of feed), which can also be linked to food intolerance. She was happy for me to continue to breastfeed for a week or two but if no weight gain occurred I was to supplement with a soy formula. I tried to breastfeed as much as possible, but Jeremy was screaming day and night and the only way I could keep him quiet for short periods was to carry him in an infant carrier on my front and to keep moving – jiggling him up and down (I believe it's known as the colic dance). We never went out.

'My other two certainly suffered: Jessica began to wet her bed and to wet at school, sometimes twice a day; Benjamin began to wake up frequently at night for cuddles. I suffered from severe and disabling migraines. We seemed to be a totally dysfunctional family. At this point the doctors offered to take Jeremy into hospital. It was not even a temptation. Fraught as we were, we were also really devoted to him. He was in so much pain most of the time, clearly so unhappy, that we could *not have left him alone on some ward to cry. Even if holding did very little to help, it felt like we were doing something.*

'I felt an awful fear – a fear that he was not and would never be normal. He did not smile at the time he should have done – he was in too much pain to smile and he did not seem to recognise us. He seemed absorbed in a world of pain.

'Our other avenue of help, when Jeremy was about eight weeks and not getting any better, was to go and see a cranial osteopath. An acquaintance at my son's nursery, having heard Jeremy's crying, came up to me and told me she had had similar problems with her little boy and that cranial osteopathy had helped. For his first treatment he would not stop screaming, so they tried to treat him while I breastfed him. I noticed no improvement until the third treatment when he did calm down quite a bit. They claimed that the moulding of the skull during childbirth affects the nerves leading into the stomach – hence the colic. However, they also advised me to try a dairy-free diet.

'In the end, Jeremy began to improve as a result, I think, of my dairy-free diet and from the supplements of soy formula: every time I tried to resume a normal diet (for a vegetarian, a lactose-free diet is very restrictive) – his colic returned with full force. The cranial osteopathy may or may not have helped, but there is no way of telling.

'Jeremy is now nine months old. He is a very happy, smiley and contented baby. We can hardly believe he is the same child.'

Anne, mother of three

30 Plan quiet evenings and try to snuggle up and have a nap with your baby during the late afternoon – a siesta can have a marked effect on your milk supply as well as your stamina, and may help ease your baby's (and your own) stress levels.

Whatever the causes of your baby's colic, once you have begun to identify a pattern it makes sense to try to be prepared so that you can give your little one extra care when he needs it. If his crying time is in the evening, for instance, try to complete as many tasks as possible during the day: make dinner in the morning, perhaps, or cook double quantities and keep extra meals handy in the freezer. You might feel more able to 'face the music' if you have everything at hand (car keys, relaxing music – whatever works for you), before the hour arrives. You might also feel more relaxed if you have a bath or shower, a quiet drink and some together-time with your partner before baby starts crying. Plan quiet evenings and try to snuggle up and have a nap with your baby during the late afternoon – a siesta can have a marked effect on your milk supply as well as your stamina, and may help ease your baby's (and your own) stress levels.

It could also be helpful to give your baby a massage and/ or a relaxation bath an hour or so before his anticipated crying time. Relaxing in a bath can help calm you as well as baby (if you feel like sharing a tub) and can help relieve tummy cramping. (For how to give a relaxation bath, see page 52.) Massage can also relieve a baby's tummy pain (see 'Massage to tame tummy troubles' on page 229). Take your cues from your baby: if he is extremely distressed or tense, it may be more helpful to gently massage his back or shoulders while cuddling him. Other soothing techniques that may help babies with colic include movement (try the 'colic carry' on page 191), and relaxing music or 'white noise', which can help babies 'tune out' to other stimuli (see 'Soothing sounds' on page 200).

31 It could be helpful to give your baby a massage and/ or a relaxation bath an hour or so before his anticipated crying time.

Some mothers report that complementary therapies such as naturopathy, aromatherapy (only for babies over three months old) and/or homoeopathy produce marked improvements in their colicky babies. (See the Resources section.)

> '*We found the spa worked best of all. Because we needed to spend hours comforting her, we would get in with her, and we were comfortable too.*'
>
> **Katrina, mother of one**

> '*Amy's colic was helped by holding a warm, wet, folded nappy against her tummy. As it cooled we would apply another one.*'
>
> **Cathy, mother of two**

Medications

As well as natural, easily performed practices such as massage, carrying and relaxation baths, there is a range of medications available to relieve crying babies when there is no medical reason for their pain. There is also a range of opinions from both parents and professionals as to the efficacy of these treatments. Before giving your baby any

such preparations – even 'natural' remedies – seek professional advice.

If your baby is fully breastfed, it is better to avoid giving
him oral medications, which can interfere with the healthy
balance of your baby's intestinal flora that is responsible
for many of the benefits of breastfeeding. Some breastfeeding mothers have found that taking herbal remedies
themselves has helped their babies, but before doing so
please consult a qualified herbalist.

Ask your pharmacist

Whether you are buying an over-the-counter remedy or
have a doctor's prescription, it's a good idea to find out as
much as you can about any medication you're buying *before*
you leave the pharmacy. In your fragile (read, confused)
state – the normal state for parents of crying babies –
these questions can also act as a double-checking precaution that you have the correct prescription and you do
understand the dosage instructions.

- What is the dosage?
- Is it best given before or after food?
- Can it be taken with other medications?
- Do I have to wake my baby for a dose during the night?

- Are there any side-effects?
- What should I do if my baby experiences side-effects?
- What should I do if my baby refuses or vomits up the medicine?

Wind and colic remedies

Some colic remedies, such as gripe water and colic drops, have been around for many years – your own mother may have used them. Some contain alcohol (for its sedative rather than medicinal effects), but as alcohol is not safe for babies always look for alcohol-free preparations. All over-the-counter products are given differing success ratings by mothers. As with any medication, read the label carefully and always follow the dosage instructions.

Colic drops: These contain an anti-flatulent which is intended to bind any tiny air bubbles together into one big bubble, the theory being that one big bubble will be easier to burp or fart!

Gripe water: Like colic drops, gripe water works on the 'wind' theory of colic. Its ingredients include dill oil (dill water is often recommended to soothe colic) and other herbal extracts. Gripe water traditionally contained alcohol – there were probably mothers who resorted to taking a swig themselves – and some brands still do, so check the label carefully and opt for a non-alcoholic version.

Homoeopathic remedies: These preparations, based on herbal and flower extracts, are available from pharmacies and health-food stores.

Milk of magnesium: Another traditional remedy, magnesium has a calming effect and enhances sleep – a bonus for parents and baby. If you use it, be careful not to exceed the dosage as too much of this mineral can cause diarrhoea. If you are breastfeeding, you can increase your baby's intake of magnesium via your breast milk by eating more magnesium-rich foods such as green leafy vegetables. However, take care with cruciferous vegetables such as cabbage, capsicum, broccoli, cauliflower, brussels sprouts and onions, as these have been associated with gas – it would be a shame to exchange one crying cause for another.

Sucking

Sucking is a comfort to babies and in helping them relax can also help soothe pain. Breastfed babies not only suck for comfort, but for an extra 'dose' of antibodies if they are exposed to illness. If you are not breastfeeding, it can be helpful to give your baby a dummy or bottle (of boiled water if he isn't hungry) when he appears to be in discomfort or distress for which there is no medical cause. But dummies have their down-sides too (for some of the pros and cons, see 'Sucking for comfort' on page 41 and 'Does your baby have a sucking problem?' on page 74).

Your baby is sweet enough!

You may find that older (or older-fashioned) mothers suggest you offer your crying baby a bottle of sugar water or formula with honey added, or a dummy dipped in honey, to encourage him to suck or to stop him crying. He does not need any such thing. Babies don't need sweetening at this age – the longer it is before they discover sweets, the longer it will be before they cry for them! And even more importantly, honey is actually a health hazard for babies under a year old (after which they seem to develop immunity): as it can contain spores of the bacterium *Clostridium botulinum*, which thrive in baby's gut and release a neurotoxin that can be deadly.

32   *Babies don't need sweetening at this age – the longer it is before they discover sweets, the longer it will be before they cry for them!*

Gastric reflux

Gastro-oesophageal reflux is the regurgitation of stomach contents into the oesophagus. Most of us experience some reflux and it usually causes no problems. While some experts believe that reflux – like colic – could be the result rather than the cause of infant distress, it is generally accepted that the process can cause heartburn-like pain, abdominal pain, and/or frequent or recurrent vomiting which may be responsible for baby distress (wriggling, squirming and 'throwing' themselves off the breast during feeding and/or screaming after feeds) and night waking.

'Katrina had silent reflux (she didn't vomit) and colic. She was born at 25 weeks gestation. She came home ten days after full term, and for the first five weeks she was a really "easy" baby. Then, she became really unsettled and niggly after feeds. From seven to nine every night, she would scream the house down. We worked as a team: my husband would make sure he was home from work and I would have dinner ready early so we could be ready for her. We would walk, sing and massage for two hours, then she would just stop and go to sleep.

'By six months, she was really niggly after feeds. The baby health nurse told us, "It's just a baby thing," and "Premmie babies can be a bit temperamental." Her crying became so

bad after each feed that I couldn't leave the house, but by the time I got to the doctor's she would be smiling. The doctor thought she may have been showing some early signs of cerebral palsy, so referred us to a paediatrician. He prescribed Mylanta in a specific dose for her size, before each milk feed. I had tried Mylanta, but I hadn't given her enough, or at every feed. By following the paediatrician's instructions, within 24 to 36 hours her pain (and crying) was all over.'

Angie, mother of two

In almost all cases, gastro-oesophageal reflux is caused by poor co-ordination or immaturity of the upper intestinal tract, with the result that the muscular tissue at the junction of the stomach and oesophagus doesn't function like a one-way valve as it is supposed to. Reflux usually disappears of its own accord as a baby matures (though an operation is needed in a very few cases).

What can you do about it?
Until your baby's system matures, understanding some basic physiology and improving the angle at which he lies and feeds may help you to relieve his distress.

After meals a baby with reflux is, theoretically at least, best put on his stomach with his head propped up at an angle of about 30 degrees, which causes the stomach to fall forward and close the opening between the stomach and the oesophagus. Remember, though, that this is only theoretical: some infants will cry if put on their stomachs, and if they cry constantly will fill their stomach with air and then start to grunt and strain for relief – this tends to make the reflux worse. (For tips to help your baby learn to enjoy 'tummy time', see page 177.)

Perhaps more important than finding the 'best' position is avoiding 'bad' positions. Young infants without much control of their abdominal or chest muscles tend to slump when they are placed in a seat. This increases the pressure in their stomachs, which tends to worsen the reflux. It can help to keep baby upright after feeds, to aid digestion: in a sling, which is comforting and leaves your hands free; or in a seat that reclines a bit. For sleeping it can also help to utilise gravity to aid digestion by raising the head end of the cot: place phone-books under the cot legs, or place a towel under the mattress (never use a pillow for a baby under twelve months). A baby hammock with an elevated head position will keep baby in a safe and comfortable sleeping position and as he stirs, may help him rock back to sleep again. If you are co-sleeping, place your baby, facing you, on his left side with his head supported in the crook of your arm.

Getting a proper diagnosis of reflux can involve a tread-mill of tests, which often simply compounds the distress (yours as well as your baby's). If other medical causes for your baby's pain have been ruled out, before you embark on more invasive testing consider whether his symptoms may in fact be due to conditions such as foremilk imbal-ance (see below), allergy or food intolerance (including reactions to foods that may pass through your breast milk). These conditions can be simply addressed by alter-ing breastfeeding practices, rather than weaning: a baby health nurse, breastfeeding counsellor or lactation con-sultant can advise you.

Lactose intolerance and foremilk imbalance

All babies are biologically designed to digest milk. From around four years of age, people from some ethnic back-grounds (non-Caucasian and non-Anglo-Saxon) can no longer do this because they stop producing the enzyme lactase, which helps the body break down lactose (a sugar present in milk). In addition, whatever their genetic her-itage some babies develop temporary lactose intolerance after a gastro-intestinal infection, while others exhibit symptoms of lactose or foremilk intolerance: spitting-up; gassiness or colic; frothy or watery, loose, green bowel motions. This is due to breastfeeding practices that result in too much lactose-rich foremilk and not enough fat-rich, hunger-satisfying hind milk.

These problems typically result from a limited time at the breast (for example, changing sides too often and/or a forceful milk ejection that causes spluttering or makes baby pull off the breast). If a baby doesn't get the hind milk, he will need to drink more (or more often) to satisfy his hunger and so consume more lactose – and if he doesn't have enough lactase he will develop symptoms similar to those of lactose intolerance: diarrhoea, which is further complicated because the milk's low fat content causes the stomach to empty rapidly; or spitting up, because the baby's stomach 'empties in the wrong direction' – when he consumes more milk than he can comfortably hold.

The solution here is to allow your baby to nurse on one breast long enough to get the hind milk, by letting him decide when he has 'finished the first breast' before you change sides. Another consideration if your baby is diagnosed with lactose intolerance is to express some foremilk until you feel your milk letting down, *before* you put him to the breast (and, of course, also let him finish the first breast first). He will then begin feeding on fattier milk and need a lower volume, which will place less stress on his digestive system until symptoms ease.

There are drops available for babies who have difficulty digesting lactose: ask your health carer whether these are relevant to your child's condition. If you are advised to wean (which is occasionally recommended as a temporary measure) but you would prefer to continue breastfeeding, seek another opinion.

Is he constipated?

Constipation is another tummy trouble which can make for a distressed baby. This problem is rare in fully breast-fed babies, because breast milk has laxative properties: it is not unusual for a breastfed baby to have frequent, runny bowel motions in the early weeks and then go for several days without a poo, and this is not a cause for concern if your baby is comfortable. If, however – whether breast- or bottle-fed – your baby strains and becomes distressed about having a bowel motion, or if he is being bottle-fed or has started on solids and has hard, dry bowel motions, do consult your doctor or baby health nurse. If constipation is the problem, offer your baby extra water to drink (this is not necessary for fully breastfed babies) and try gently massaging around his tummy in clockwise circles to stimulate elimination of waste from the bowel. If constipation persists in your bottle-fed baby, ask your doctor or baby health nurse whether you should change formulas. For babies over six months old, diluted prune or apple juice (check with your baby health nurse) can help keep fluid inside his intestines and soften the stools.

If your baby screams as he uses his bowels, and you notice specks of fresh blood in his poo, his pain may be caused by a fissure (a small ulcerated sore) on the edge of his anus. (You can see this if you lift his legs gently.) An anal fissure may be caused by constipation and certainly will not heal easily if your baby is constipated. To aid healing, remember how you healed your own perineum after birth: sit baby for a few minutes in a shallow basin – the bathroom sink will do – of warm salted water after he has used his bowels, then gently pat the area dry (or use a hairdryer on 'Warm') and apply a healing ointment such as zinc and castor-oil cream (see 'Lotions and potions' on page 125).

33 *If constipation is the problem, offer your baby extra water to drink (this is not necessary for fully breastfed babies) and try gently massaging around his tummy in clockwise circles to stimulate elimination of waste from the bowel.*

Food allergies and intolerance

If you or your partner suffer from allergies such as eczema, asthma or hayfever, or if there is a family history of such conditions, it is more likely that your baby will do so too. If this is the case, it is worth considering whether excessive crying may be linked to a food sensitivity.

Allergies and food intolerance in infants may cause a wide range of symptoms including tummy cramps, nausea, vomiting, gastric reflux, silent reflux and breast refusal, frequent night waking, wheezing, dermatitis and rashes. However, before you conclude that any symptoms are allergy-related, other medical causes should be ruled out for your baby's discomfort. The best way to protect your baby from allergies is to breastfeed exclusively for the first six months. Food allergies in exclusively breast-fed babies are caused by foods that pass into your milk, not by the milk itself. Some sensitive babies react even to small amounts of some foods in breast milk: the most common culprit is cows-milk protein (milk, cheese, yoghurt), though chocolate, peanuts, eggs, fish, wheat and citrus can also cause reactions.

Salicylates are chemicals that occur naturally in foods such as fruits, fruit juices, vegetables, herbs, spices, nuts, wines, tea and coffee. They are also present in food colourings and additives, and can trigger food intolerance symptoms in sensitive people. Babies who are sensitive to these chemicals may be restless and cry a lot. If you suspect food intolerance in your breastfeeding baby, you might like to first try avoiding foods with additives, such as soft drinks (see 'Food intolerance' in the Resources section). Some people find that cutting down is enough, but if you still have problems, especially if there are family members with food intolerance symptoms like migraine, you might want to try an elimination diet. Because this is a complex and stressful process, it is essential to be supervised by a dietician.

'There is nothing more isolating than a baby who screams and vomits – there are no offers to hold the baby! I would walk into the doctors' with this chubby, thriving looking baby and of course, it would look as though I was simply a neurotic mother. Eventually, through trial and error, I discovered that he seemed sensitive to salicylates: when I stopped eating apples he calmed down significantly. A dietician supervised my

elimination diet while I continued to breastfeed. My son is now 13 and has no allergies, but is on a strict elimination diet under supervision of a dietician because food additives have such a detrimental effect on his behaviour.'

Glenda, mother of two

Before eliminating foods from your diet, it is worth examining your baby's feeding pattern (see 'Lactose intolerance and foremilk imbalance' above). If, however, you think that the crying seems to be related to feeds, jot down his crying times and what you have eaten: if there appears to be a link, one simple solution is to eliminate the suspect food for at least a week (preferably two). If your baby's symptoms disappear, avoid the suspect food in future; or reintroduce a small amount of it into your diet – if symptoms reappear, you can be pretty certain you have nailed the culprit. It can take several weeks for eliminating foods to make a difference, but if the result calms your baby (and you), modifying your diet is a small sacrifice.

34   *If, however, you think that the crying seems to be related to feeds, jot down his crying times and what you have eaten: if there appears to be a link, one simple solution is to eliminate the suspect food for at least a week (preferably two).*

If you are bottle-feeding, it may be recommended that you change to a soy-milk formula. Be aware, though, that about 50 per cent of infants who are allergic to cows-milk protein are also allergic to soy protein, so it may not necessarily be helpful to race out and buy soy-milk formula. You could try changing formulas for a week and see if it makes a difference – your baby might be in the group that will benefit! Hypo-allergenic formulas are available, and are recommended by the American Academy of Paediatrics as the first preference for sensitive babies, rather than soy formula, which has also raised concerns among some professionals that the high phyto-oestrogen levels may have detrimental effects on baby boys. Hypo-allergenic formula, such as Neo-cate, can be purchased at pharmacies, but is expensive without a prescription. Consult with your baby health nurse and/or your doctor before changing formulas.

When your baby is ready to start solids, don't be in too much of a rush to turn him into a gourmet. Introduce foods one at a time in small amounts (see the chapter 'Is she hungry?') and, if you have a family history of allergies, don't offer potential allergens until your baby is a year old. If he has been breastfed, he will have already experienced a variety of flavours through your milk, so introducing new foods is likely to be easier.

Fags, booze and other vices

Parental smoking is linked to a higher incidence of infant colic, and in rare cases may cause nausea, vomiting, abdominal pain and diarrhoea in breastfed babies. While studies show that the risk of colic is increased whichever parent smokes, rather than resulting from a transfer of chemicals through the mother's milk, heavy smoking (more than 20 a day) has been shown to reduce a mother's milk supply, probably because smoking lowers her level of prolactin, the hormone that aids relaxation and milk flow. If you can't give up, at least try to cut down and do smoke outside, away from your baby.

35 *The risk of colic is increased if either parent smokes.*

On the whole, motherhood and alcohol aren't very compatible. Whether you are breastfeeding or not, alcohol will reduce your own alertness and responsiveness to your baby, which could result in unnecessary crying (by your baby) as well as impaired ability to handle emergencies (by you). Also, if you have abstained during pregnancy, you will be a cheap drunk for a while – it will take a lot less alcohol to affect you.

At the time of writing, the National Health and Medical Research Council is revising safe drinking guidelines and it looks as though pregnant and breastfeeding women will be advised not to drink alcohol at all. This is because, in light of worldwide research, a safe limit of alcohol consumption can't be determined during pregnancy and breastfeeding – there are potential risks to babies, whose immature livers aren't able to process the alcohol transmitted through the placenta or their mother's milk.

Daily consumption of alcohol by breastfeeding mothers has been shown to affect baby's sleep patterns (with babies falling asleep more quickly but waking more often – and crying), increase the risk of slow weight gain and slow gross motor development.

Although many people may tell you that a glass of alcohol will increase your milk supply, there is evidence that this isn't the case. Drinking more than two standard drinks can inhibit your letdown and even small doses of alcohol can alter the taste of breast-milk. Babies dislike this, so may not drain the breast. These factors could temporarily reduce your milk supply – and result in more tears. An inadequately drained breast can also increase the likelihood of mastitis.

If you do choose to drink while you are breastfeeding, it is important to be aware that alcohol will pass into your milk very easily – as your blood alcohol level rises, so does the level of alcohol in your breast milk. The good news is that as your blood alcohol level drops, so does the level of alcohol in your milk.

Alcohol peaks in your blood approximately half an hour to an hour after drinking (this varies among individuals, depending on factors such as how much food was eaten in the same time period, your body weight and percentage of body fat). It takes approximately two hours for your body to break down one standard drink and your blood alcohol level to drop to zero (two standard drinks will take four hours).

If you plan to drink while you are breastfeeding, either express *before* drinking and feed your baby 'alcohol-free' milk or drink *after* a feed and wait until your blood alcohol level is safe before you breastfeed again.

Whether you are breastfeeding or not, if you drink it is wise to have a designated parent (one parent stays sober and in charge of the baby) just as you would have a designated driver.

Although you may feel in need of a caffeine hit to help you cope with a crying baby, if you are breastfeeding this could be the very reason he is irritable. Although one or two cups of coffee a day probably won't affect a baby, a newborn can take almost 100 hours to metabolise the caffeine in a single cup of coffee, so the caffeine he gets through your milk can accumulate. And don't forget that caffeine is also found in cola drinks, chocolate and, in smaller amounts, tea (including Asian green tea). It is easy to create a vicious circle: baby cries, you drink more coffee, he cries more, and downward you spiral. Caffeine has no nutritional value so why not consider cutting it out altogether and trying decaf, herbal teas or a coffee substitute, especially if you managed without it during pregnancy.

> **36** *Although you may feel in need of a caffeine hit to help you cope with a crying baby, if you are breastfeeding this could be the very reason he is irritable.*

Teething

Although lots of babies are barely bothered by teeth erupting, the experience can turn others (even if they are normally the most placid beings) into little aliens who cry, develop sleep problems and want to breastfeed more frequently for comfort. Some babies may refuse to feed, or may bite down hard with their sensitive gums – strangely, biting seems to bring some relief.

If your baby won't feed, you could try nursing when he has fallen asleep – just pick him up gently without waking him and hold him to the breast. If you are concerned about his fluid intake, offer home-made icypoles made from expressed breast milk, formula (if you are bottle-feeding) or diluted fruit juice.

Ask your doctor or pharmacist about teething reme-dies. Meanwhile, try some of the following tips for easing painful gums:

- Rub baby's gums with your finger (wash your hands thoroughly first).
- Chill a teething ring in the freezer (don't ever hang a teething ring around your baby's neck, as the cord is a strangling hazard).
- Let him chew on a wet washcloth, or a frozen piece of apple inside a muslin cloth (to prevent choking on chewed-off pieces of apple – although he doesn't yet have teeth, he's about to!)
- If baby has started eating solids, he may enjoy chilled soft foods such as a frozen slice of banana, which will mush down as he gnaws on it (with supervision, of

course), or try icy-cold apple purée. Never give hard foods such as carrot, which may be a choking hazard as those teeth emerge and bite little pieces off.

'Teething was nightmarish. We tried the usual: a commercial teething gel (available from pharmacies), paracetamol, lemon juice on the gums, icicles to suck, and lots of rocking in the pram, even at times with a hotpack under his cheek.'

Amy, mother of one

37 *If you are concerned about his fluid intake, offer home-made icypoles made from expressed breast milk, formula (if you aren't breastfeeding) or diluted fruit juice.*

Nappy rash

Just as chafed red skin can make an adult miserable, so nappy rash makes for an unhappy, crying baby. You will know for certain if your baby has nappy rash. His bottom will no longer be as smooth as a baby's bottom should be, but red and inflamed instead; and he will cry or be irritable, particularly when urine scalds his sore behind. Although babies with very sensitive skin or a family history of skin disorders such as eczema or psoriasis may be more prone to nappy rash, the reality is that any baby is a candidate and keeping your baby's bottom clean and dry is the best preventive strategy.

There are a few special circumstances which may make your baby more prone to nappy rash. If he has diarrhoea or a fungal infection, for instance, he will probably have a sore bottom as well. Food allergies may also be a cause of nappy rash. Meanwhile, wash your hands before and after nappy changes, keep baby as dry as possible, use a barrier cream, or a healing cream if he has a rash, and see your doctor if baby develops a rash that doesn't heal in a day or two.

Rash decisions

It may seem obvious to say 'change your baby frequently', but in practice this doesn't always happen. Perhaps the definition of 'often' is relative, especially if you are using disposables or plastic pants: baby's bottom may seem dry to you and disposables do seem to absorb a lot of wee, but somewhere in that bundle is a whole lot of moisture and – particularly in hot weather – the plastic casing and the layers of whatever it is that holds the sogginess don't allow your baby's skin to 'breathe'. This warm, moist environment makes delicate baby skin vulnerable to damage by irritants and to infections such as thrush. So even if you are using 'super-absorbent' disposable nappies, you need to change them every time they are wet or dirty, or feel heavy even if they don't seem to be saturated.

Conditions such as diarrhoea and fungal infections can also be a result of treatment with antibiotics, which can upset the flora in baby's gut and allow yeast-based organisms to thrive. When these are eventually excreted into a warm, moist nappy, they also thrive on baby's delicate skin. If your baby develops diarrhoea as a side-effect of antibiotics, ask your doctor for an alternative medication. Fungal and bacterial infections should be treated by a doctor.

If your baby is allergic to something he has eaten, the rash may appear as a red ring around his anus. When you eliminate the offending food from his diet – and/or yours, if you are breastfeeding – this will clear.

> **38**   *If your baby is allergic to something he has eaten, the rash may appear as a red ring around his anus. When you eliminate the offending food from his diet – and/or yours, if you are breastfeeding – this will clear.*

What you can do

If you are using cloth nappies, keep moisture away from baby's skin by using nappy liners. Some (such as the

Bobaby brand) are made of a thin knitted fabric which draws moisture away from baby's skin. (Bobaby also make bibs and singlets that prevent irritation of delicate skin, and are especially recommended for babies with eczema.) These liners are excellent for night-time and if you use them you don't need a nappy cream.

To minimise irritation, wash cloth nappies in pure soap flakes if possible, or soak in a commercial soaker, then simply rinse and spin before drying. Thorough rinsing is important, as detergent residue may irritate your baby's skin: adding 3 tablespoons of vinegar to every 4 litres of water in the final rinse will reduce the alkali levels which foster the activity of the enzymes in baby poo that 'attack' your baby's delicate skin – the combination of a wet and dirty nappy is a potent cause of nappy rash.

Wipe-out!

To reduce the likelihood of nappy rash, when you change your baby wipe his bottom firmly but gently from front to back (this is especially important for girls, as germs from faeces can otherwise be transmitted to the vagina). Make sure you wipe and dry well all the cracks and crevices, and dry baby's bottom thoroughly before you put on a clean nappy. There is no need to pull back a boy's foreskin, but if your baby girl has had a bowel motion you may have to gently part the labia and carefully wipe from top to bottom, using a clean cloth for each 'wipe'.

An easy way to clean a baby after a bowel motion is to dunk your cherub's bottom into a hand-basin of warm water. This is also a useful tactic if he already has a rash, as wiping will simply cause more friction – and possibly more crying. If he is so sore that he screams when you put his bottom in water (such as when you try to bath him), try applying sorbolene cream (available from supermarkets and chemists) before you put him in the water, or forgo the bath and try pouring a mixture of sorbolene and water over his bottom from a jug.

Avoid perfumed wipes, cleansers and soaps, and wipes that contain spirit: these remove the natural oil from a baby's skin, may irritate and will almost certainly aggravate nappy rash. A thick, warm, wet face-washer will undoubtedly feel much nicer on his bottom than a thin cold wipe, and is just as convenient to carry with you. You just need access to a hot-water tap (don't forget to carry a plastic bag for soiled cloths). Some mothers who use cloth nappies at home opt for disposables and disposable wipes for outings.

39   *An easy way to clean your cherub after a bowel motion is to dunk his bottom into a hand-basin of warm water.*

Avoid friction

Clothes or nappies that rub – tight outer clothing such as jumpsuits, a loose cloth nappy or a disposable of the incorrect size – can damage soggy skin and make it more vulnerable to infection. This is why you may notice a rash on your baby's buttocks while the creases of his groin are unaffected. And when you put on cloth nappies, remember to put the pin in horizontally – pins that point up or down will poke into baby and may prick him (and make him yell!) if they come undone. Of course, you can use modern cloth nappies that fasten without pins.

Lotions and potions

Along with nappy-free kicks in the sun and regular nappy changes, barrier creams help prevent nappy rash. Fads and fashions abound: some mothers swear by good old-fashioned petroleum jelly, or zinc and castor-oil cream, while others go for the latest products. A couple of popular brands to look for are Lansinoh or Marcalan, which are hypo-allergenic, purified lanolin (which you can also use on your nipples); and Aromababy nappy balm or cream (again, some mothers swear by this as a moisturiser for themselves!), which has a good reputation among parents of eczema babies.

Check the labels and bypass any creams containing potential allergens or pesticides. Peanut-oil-based creams may cause an allergic reaction, and pawpaw cream – once a popular cure-all – is now suspect since pawpaw crops receive a fair dose of chemical spray. Bear in mind also that pawpaw was traditionally used as a meat tenderiser and also to debride wounds, so is not recommended on babies' bottoms or mothers' nipples. Products containing mineral oils can clog baby's pores and have been associated with child poisoning when older babies have managed to remove lids, so look for products based on vegetable oils and without chemical additives or perfumes. Also avoid talcum powder, as it tends to become soggy and hold moisture against baby's skin, particularly in crevices (and may anyway be inhaled).

40 Nothing beats nappy-free kicks in the fresh air for preventing or healing nappy rash.

Nappy-free

In some cultures, of course, babies don't wear nappies at all. A mother usually carries her baby in a sling and is so attuned to his body language that she simply holds him out when he needs to wee or poo. There is a movement in some non-traditional societies that advocates EC (elimination communication) as a parenting practice: its proponents maintain this is not about early toilet training but rather about being aware of a baby's body language and following his lead – they find they only put nappies on their babies for outings or night-time. EC adherents claim that learning even very young babies' elimination signals is no more difficult than, say, being aware of hunger cues. Even if you find this approach a bit far out, if your baby has a rash it will help to leave him nappy-free as much as possible. If the room is warm, you could leave his bottom bare during daytime naps as well: lay him on a towel, a folded cloth nappy or a bunny rug to protect the bedding.

Chapter five
Solving the sleep puzzle

Like a zombie, you are staggering about in the wee small hours (and much of the day too) wondering whether a DNA test for maternity is in order: you spent weeks lovingly decorating your baby's room and she doesn't seem to have inherited a single gene that reflects your passion for matching linen sets – unless she is in your arms or snuggled against your warm body, she protests by crying.

Not so long ago, even after several nights burning the midnight oil, you could at least refill your sleep bank with an early night once in a while. The most trying aspect of the utter exhaustion you are now experiencing is that it won't simply disappear after a good night's sleep – because 'a good night's sleep' and a baby aren't the most compatible pair, at least not in the early weeks.

It simply isn't worth trying to make your baby's sleeps fit your own schedule – this way leads to frustration and unhappiness for everyone involved. A baby's sleep patterns are quite different to ours: not only do babies take longer to fall asleep in the first place (which means you have to help them do so) but they arouse more easily and spend twice as much time in light (active) sleep as we do. Premature babies spend even more time in light sleep than full-term babies, so if you have a premature baby you can expect sleepless nights and 'catnap' days for even longer. Sorry, but there is nothing like realistic expectations to prevent disappointment!

It may be of little comfort as your baby's crying has you crawling from your bed yet again, but her light sleep is actually assisting her brain development: during REM (rapid eye movement) sleep, nerve proteins, the building blocks of the brain, are produced and blood flows to the brain at nearly twice the rate than during deep sleep. As described in 'Crying times' (see page 13), babies who have been sleeping quite peacefully for weeks or even months tend to become wakeful as they enter into a new stage of physical, neurological or emotional development. And when you combine several factors – teething, say, plus separation anxiety (see page 16), beginning to crawl, and a greater awareness of the world around them, it is really no wonder that many babies around five or six months old suddenly become unsettled at night.

If you have a wakeful, crying baby, it is easy to be enticed by the idea of training her to sleep via such techniques as 'controlled crying' – especially when you're told that if you don't she will be getting you out of bed every night until she leaves home. In fact, babies' sleep patterns may not only make them smarter but also help protect them against some forms of **SIDS** (sudden infant death syndrome): they will arouse easily if there is a breathing obstruction or if they are too hot or cold, both of which are **SIDS** risk factors.

41 *A baby's sleep patterns are quite different to ours: not only do babies take longer to fall asleep in the first place (which means you have to help them do so) but they arouse more easily.*

'We did go to a sleeping class to learn how to help our baby sleep, since they really haven't had to worry about day and night before. Some of it made sense, some seemed quite archaic. The controlled crying thing didn't make any sense to us at all. Why let your child cry for a controlled period, when they are obviously crying for a valid reason. I can understand that they need to learn to help themselves to get to sleep and put themselves back to sleep but to leave them for such a long time without that support, I personally couldn't stand to hear my child in such a stressful rage that they were almost turning

blue. I would have to cuddle and hold and love, to let them know that Dad can help.'

Sam, father of one

'Right from the beginning Dan and I had not felt at all comfortable with the concept of "control crying". I had read The Continuum Concept *by Jean Liedloff and been so haunted by the chapter describing the western model of infant sleep practices that I was determined to never find myself doing "that" to my precious baby. For the first few weeks, I was more than happy to feed and rock him to sleep – as long as I felt comfortable doing this, it was okay, right? However, since he was a colicky baby it was never as easy as a little feed and a little rock and off he would go. The feeding and rocking would go on for hours and eventually I became really exhausted and started to doubt my technique.*

'Like any new mum, I began to ask others what they did to get their babies to sleep in an effort to find a better way. I remember very vividly a phone conversation I had with a girlfriend of mine at the time. She had also had sleep difficulties with her daughter, who was a few months older than our baby, and in her efforts to cope had ended up in a sleep clinic. They had taught her all the procedures – of wrapping the baby, turning her away from you and of leaving the baby to cry for set

periods of time. She swore to me that it had changed her life and almost begged me to do the same. She was so determined in her argument – I felt like she was almost trying to sell me the idea – it was as though if I took on the practice with my child, she could feel justified in her decision to deprive her baby also. I insisted that it was not for me and as she hung up I swear I almost felt a sense of pity in her voice. It was as if she believed I was denying myself this wonderful opportunity to be free of struggle – when, in actual fact, all I could see was this glaring example of deprivation and cruelty taking place.'

Jane, mother of one

'My first baby, had to sleep in his room, not ours, and I had to get up for all his feeds and stay in there for all the settling. No doubt this contributed to my exhaustion, but I believed that it was what you should do. Next baby, eighteen months later: basinet in our room, feeds in bed and falls asleep. Eventually baby was moved into his own room. Now with another baby, only eight weeks old: starts off in his bed in our room, ends up in our bed. Sleep is so essential for coping with life. Unfortunately for a lot of us, it takes our own experiences to grow from and become more confident parents. Now, I don't even bother to check how long it is between feeds: if Angus cries he gets fed, I don't have time to do controlled crying. I spent

so much time teaching my first to sleep, I wished I'd spent it enjoying him.'

Megan, mother of three

For all babies, reaching the point where they 'sleep through' is a developmental process – just like eating solid foods or learning to use the toilet – and, just like these processes, cannot be hastened and may in fact be delayed by worry or pressure. All babies do eventually sleep through – though it has to be pointed out that in most research studies 'through the night' is defined as *five* hours.

If you are thinking that even *five* hours sleep in a row sounds like a dream come true, take heart: there are some things you can do to help your baby (and you) sleep better. After all, if you are exhausted you will be less able to wake up yourself and attend to your baby when you need to, and this isn't a safe option. (For some tips on alleviating exhaustion, see the chapter 'Coping (and not coping) with the crying'. For more specific information about sleeping, read my book *Sleeping Like a Baby*)

Meanwhile, instead of letting frustration affect your relationship with your baby, try to see those little night howls in a positive light – as an opportunity for one more cuddle with your little one. All too soon, this *will* pass. I promise!

42 *Instead of letting frustration affect your relationship with your baby, try to see those little night howls in a positive light– as an opportunity for one more cuddle with your little one.*

Helping her get to sleep…

Of course, you have to actually get your baby to sleep in the first place, and this can be difficult if she is upset, especially if her fractiousness and your own tension are becoming a vicious circle. And not all sleep difficulties are night-time events: babies can also be unsettled and cry during the day if they are having difficulty getting to sleep, or if they are overtired, overstimulated or generally feeling out of sorts. This can impact not only on your own wellbeing but on your baby's ability to unwind and sleep at night as well.

The magic touch

Thanks to an early reflex, for the first couple of months you can use this little trick to help calm a crying spell or to encourage sleep. Gently stroke your baby's forehead with the side of your finger, right down the middle to the bridge of her nose. Magic! She will automatically close her eyes. It is best to try this once she has calmed down, not while she is at full bellow, but it may well soothe her long enough to stop a crying spell in its tracks.

Bedtime rituals

Evening rituals can become cues that gently help even tiny babies wind down and become conditioned to sleep. If you can get your baby used to being lulled to sleep by Dad as well as Mum, then you can take turns.

From the earliest days, give her a relaxation bath in the evening, just before bedtime (for instructions, see page 52). You can gradually introduce other sleep signals and a bedtime routine, including one or more of the following in any order that works for you:

- a massage and/or a bath (perhaps with a few drops of relaxing lavender oil for babies over three months old)
- a cuddle
- some gentle music or a song
- a story
- a prayer or meditation
- a feed

43 *From the earliest days, give her a relaxation bath in the evening, just before bedtime (for instructions, see page 52). You can gradually introduce other sleep signals and a bedtime routine.*

Just a word of caution: don't make your bedtime routine too complicated. As a rule of thumb, don't use any tricks you (or an unwitting babysitter) are not prepared to perform every night for several years! Try to keep bedtime play gentle, and turn off television and loud music. It can be a good idea to give her evening feed in the bedroom. (If you have been out and she has fallen asleep in the car, simply put her to bed as quietly as possible.)

Another thing to consider is the difference between snuggling next to a warm body and being placed between cold sheets. While you should be careful never to overheat your baby, her bed will be more inviting in cool weather if you warm the mattress to body temperature with a hot-water bottle before you put her in.

'We try to make a very calm environment for Annalise to go to sleep in at night. A nice warm bath, some classical lullaby music, a warm bottle, a big quiet hug from Mum and Dad, and she usually goes off to sleep fairly quickly. That could all change next week, though. This week she likes to have a small soft toy with her when she first nods off. We take it out of the cot later. You need to be flexible and try things. Listen to other people's experiences, but remember it is not them up at 2 a.m. trying to get your little one to sleep. Do what suits you and you

partner and remember all children are different. I also look at it from a standpoint that if she knows that Dad or Mum will comfort her when things seem bad now, she will come to us in the future when she is 5, 9, 16, 21, 40. Whatever age, she needs to know that there will always be Mum's or Dad's shoulder to cry and be supported on. But she also needs to know that she will develop the confidence to be able to sort out problems, how ever big or small, for herself with that support for backup.'

Tony, father of one

44 *While you should be careful never to overheat your baby, her bed will be more inviting in cool weather if you warm the mattress to body temperature with a hot-water bottle before you put her in.*

Falling asleep at the breast

Despite the advice you're almost sure to hear to the contrary, there is nothing wrong with letting your baby fall asleep at your breast. In fact, the hormones produced by breastfeeding help you relax and have a soporific effect on her. It makes no sense for you to resist this calming process, or to wake your baby when she has finally fallen asleep. Doing so could even inhibit your milk let-down, resulting in a lower fat content and thus a hungry baby who wakes after a shorter time. All in all, if you are happy breastfeeding your baby day and night, whatever her age, this is fine – she will eventually outgrow this need, even if you do absolutely nothing to speed things up.

45 *There is nothing wrong with letting your baby fall asleep at your breast. In fact, the hormones produced by breastfeeding help you relax and have a soporific effect on your baby.*

Bear in mind that if your baby wakes and cries during the night she will expect to be soothed back to sleep with whatever sleep cues she has been taught. If she becomes accustomed to being breastfed to sleep, and if on waking will only settle again with a feed, when she is a few months old you can gently teach her to go to sleep without the breast if this is an issue for you. Rather than resort to a cold-turkey ('let her cry it out') approach, it is kinder for you as well as your baby to approach this in gradual stages:

🌼 For a week, feed her a little earlier in the evening and then rock her to sleep in your arms (or Dad's).

Throughout this transition, feed her back to sleep as usual when she wakes at night.

🌿 Once you have broken the association between feeding and bedtime, you can shorten the rocking period and try putting your baby into bed when she is calm though still awake. You may also find that playing calming music will help (see 'Soothing sounds' on page 200).

Once your baby learns to go to sleep without a feed, she will naturally be able to fall asleep again by herself if she wakes during the night and you will also be able to put her to bed in the daytime too without feeding her to sleep. Remember, though, that hunger and thirst are affected by factors such as the weather, your baby's activity levels, growth spurts and impending illness, so please be flexible. Any changes like these are best made gradually, with love, to avoid confusion and stress to your baby – she doesn't understand why you have chosen to change the rules. It is also wise to consider that resistance (in the form of more crying) may be an indication of a strong need that is not being met. Be sensitive to your baby's responses.

'I was very relieved when they [a mother–baby unit] were able to take me in for a five-day stay. The nurse I spoke to was lovely

and assured me that I just needed to learn the techniques and my baby would be sleeping through the night in three days. This turned into farce when after three nights of rocking the cot for hours the staff assured me that although he was a much more difficult case, he'd be sleeping through by the end of the week. At the end of the five days, I was sent home with the advice that if I continued the techniques at home and was really, really consistent he would sleep through very soon. Despite the fact that I never again fed him between 11 p.m. and 5 a.m., he didn't sleep through the night for the first time until he was ten months old. All that rocking, when a few minutes of breastfeeding every hour or two would have got him back to sleep.'

Lexi, mother of one

46   *Any changes to bedtime practices are best made gradually, with love, to avoid confusion and stress to your baby–she doesn't understand why you have chosen to change the rules.*

… and to stay asleep

'Sleeping like a baby' can mean interruptions by little night howls for several months or longer. An Australian study that looked at more than 3000 children in the first months after birth found that nearly all the babies woke at least once per night, with more than 5 per cent waking at least five times. At three months, two-thirds of the babies were still waking regularly but at four months, half of the babies were sleeping through (in infant sleep studies, 'all night' means five hours). However, a very large percentage of babies in the study began waking again, with just under two-thirds of babies aged ten to twelve months regularly waking. At this age, 12.5 per cent were waking three or more times a night. So if those inadequate feelings emerge ('What am I doing wrong?') it might help to accept that your baby's cries in the night are more normal than exceptional. Of course, simply knowing that you are not alone listening to little night howls will not solve your sleep problem. However, there are ways to minimise waking once your baby falls asleep.

Shhh, is she really asleep?

Your baby has fallen asleep in your arms or at your breast and you have ever so gently slipped her into bed and tiptoed out of the room, but just a few minutes later she has woken – yelling again. This is possibly because she was only in a light sleep state when you put her down: the secret is to wait until her limbs are completely limp before you move her – when an arm droops and flops, she is in a deeper sleep state and so should (there are never any guarantees, only high hopes) stay asleep. To make sure, as you transfer her to bed, keep one hand on her for a few moments rather than trying to make a quick getaway. A few extra minutes in the first place will often save you a lot of frustrating effort later.

Awake again

You know your baby was sound asleep when you put him down – his limbs were limp and he seemed completely out to it, but still he wakes moments later. This can be fairly typical behaviour for a baby who has a strong startle reflex – despite being sound asleep when you popped him down, the change in position onto his back triggers his startle reflex, he jerks and/or smacks himself in the face (not realising it is his own hand that has walloped him!) and he wakes and cries. This sudden waking is also quite common for babies who have gastric reflux (see page 104). These babies often cry with discomfort when they are laid flat to sleep or for a nappy change.

Because it isn't always easy to determine exactly what is causing your soundly sleeping baby to cry out just moments after he is put down, you could try a 'blanket approach' – literally. Make up your baby's bed with the head elevated and a Safe T Sleep baby wrap in place (see Resources). Wrap your baby in a soft blanket or muslin sheet (if the weather is warm) before you settle him, play some gentle music and hold him either until he is drowsy or asleep (rock or feed if this works for you), then gently place him into bed. To stop baby sliding downwards and also to help him feel securely contained, fasten the Safe T Sleep around your wrapped baby. This will stop him sliding down in his bed and will also hold him secure (much like he would be in your arms) so that he isn't disturbed if he startles. If reflux or wind are waking your little one, raising his head will help avert discomfort – and crying!

Encourage daytime feeds and night-time sleep

At about two months, most babies settle into having one longer sleep period: if this is during the day, it is logical that they may need more feeds during the night. Older babies, who tend to be too busy crawling and exploring during the day to feed properly, may also get their feed/wake cycles out of kilter and be hungry during the night. It makes sense after the early weeks of adjustment, to gradually help your baby shift into a more convenient (for you) feeding and sleeping cycle, by encouraging her to feed more during the day so that she might have the longer sleep at night.

If your baby goes more than four hours between feeds during the day, try gently waking her, changing her nappy and offering a feed. If she is unwilling to feed, though, respect her pattern for now and try again another time: attempting to make your baby fit a rigid routine could actually delay her body adjusting naturally to a normal day/night rhythm. You can also try offering a cluster of feeds closer together in the evening – it is normal for some babies to feed frequently in the evening anyway, as if they are 'tanking up' for the night.

Another strategy is to offer a top-up feed just before you go to bed yourself, regardless of when your baby last fed. This may just give your baby the extra calories she needs to sleep a bit longer. If you do try this, make it a 'dream feed': if baby has already been asleep for a couple of hours, don't wake her, don't turn on the lights and don't change her nappy unless absolutely necessary. Simply pick her up gently and hold a nipple (breast or bottle) against her lips. She will automatically suck and there will be no need to burp her (which is sure to wake her) – she will be so relaxed that she won't swallow much air anyway. (If you are breastfeeding, the top-up should be a breastfeed as formula may upset her tummy and will reduce the protective effects of breastfeeding.)

47   *Offer a top-up feed just before you go to bed yourself, regardless of when your baby last fed. This may just give your baby the extra calories she needs to sleep a bit longer.*

'I give Molly her last bottle for the night just before I go to bed at around 11 p.m., and she usually sleeps till around seven. I don't even wake her or change her nappy. Last night, we tried to see how long she would sleep if we didn't "top her up". She was wide awake at two in the morning, crying for a feed, then she wanted to play. There was no way we could get her to go back to sleep.'

Dave, father of a four-month-old

Help her to know day from night

A study at Fukishima University in Japan asked mothers of newborns to track their babies' sleep behaviour for six months. They found that for the first few weeks babies were as likely to be awake in the dark as in the daylight hours. At seven weeks, almost all the babies shifted to sleeping more at night than during the day. By twelve weeks, most (though not all) had consolidated their sleep into naps and rarely woke for long periods at night, although many still woke to feed.

You can't force your baby to learn the difference between day and night. However, many parents find that emphasising the differences can help alter their baby's rhythm so she learns that night is for sleeping. This doesn't mean not attending to your baby at night, it simply means being more 'boring' by keeping the lights dim for night feeds and saving playtime and noise for daylight hours. Some parents also find it helpful to leave the curtains open both day and night so that their baby's circadian rhythm (the internal body clock that tells us when to wake and sleep) can adjust. Spending time outdoors during the day also helps night-time sleep, and although Grandma will swear it is the fresh air that makes the difference it is likely that exposure to sunlight helps babies tune into the difference between day and night. It will also help your baby's internal clock to adapt, and help her fall asleep more easily, if you put her to bed at the same time each night.

As your baby grows, another way of discouraging her from waking up completely during night feeds is to avoid changing her nappy during the feed unless it is really necessary. If she does need a change, it is better to do it before or halfway through the feed rather than disturb her with cold air on her bottom when she is content and groggily full.

However, please don't be too hard on yourself if you find yourself enjoying some midnight 'goo-ing' and 'gaa-ing' with your little one – you have a right to enjoy any smiles your baby gives you. And be patient: whatever you do, her internal body clock won't be fully developed until at *least* six weeks and more likely not until around twelve to fifteen weeks.

48 *You can't force your baby to learn the difference between day and night, but many parents find that emphasising the differences can help alter their baby's rhythm so she learns that night is for sleeping.*

'I used a bedside lamp so the lighting was always dim for night feeds and I was quieter than during the day, but although I was told I was reinforcing my baby's night-time waking, I couldn't resist a little play. At night, I got those gorgeous smiles all to myself. During the day, I was always so aware of my toddler's needs that I wasn't quite as focused on my baby. And it didn't matter anyway. He started sleeping a long stretch at just eight weeks. I felt like running around the block and shouting, because my first baby woke until he was almost two (years!) even though I followed all the "rules".'

Sarah, mother of two

Peaceful days make peaceful nights

If your baby cries or is very wakeful during the night, or is grizzly and has difficulty winding down in the evening, it may help to assess what is happening during the day. Are you busy and rushing around, and as a result either disturbing her daytime sleeps so she is becoming over-tired or perhaps transferring your own stress to her? Are you spending enough time playing and interacting with her during the daytime, or is she spending long periods 'amusing herself'? Could time in child-care mean she needs to stoke up on 'Mummy time' at night? Is the household under stress from factors such as moving, visitors, illness, relationship problems?

Just as babies need a certain amount of nutrition, they also have a cuddle requirement, and if this isn't met during the day they are likely to need extra loving at night. They are also like little super-sensitive radars picking up on all the emotions flowing around them, so their behaviour will often be like a barometer of your own feelings: even when you think your feelings are safely tucked away inside, you may find your baby shedding the tears you are holding back. The best solution is to take time to give your baby plenty of attention, carrying and playing with her during the day and providing a calm, stress-free environment so that her emotional tank – as well as her tummy – is full.

> **49** *Take time to give your baby plenty of attention, carrying and playing with her during the day and providing a calm, stress-free environment so that her emotional tank – as well as her tummy – is full.*

Overtired or overstimulated?

Sometimes your baby's crying may be a way of releasing pent-up stress. This is especially common in the evening after a busy day, at which times, it is best to let her cry rather than trying to bombard her with further stimulation in an effort to divert a crying spell. This doesn't mean leaving her alone to 'cry it out': it simply means being calm yourself – often easier said than done, I know, but try taking some deep, slow breaths and relaxing your shoulders and arms (so she won't feel your tension) – and limiting stimulation while you hold her until she feels better. (Some babies prefer to be put down in times like these.) Just as we usually feel better after a good cry, this is often the case for a baby who is crying to release stress.

Or her crying may be an effort to tune out excessive stimuli. We tend to interpret advice to give our babies an interesting environment to mean we have to constantly play with and stimulate them. This isn't the case: in fact babies need quiet times to explore their own bodies and the world around them, to learn to direct their own learning without distractions, and simply to rest and rejuvenate without people 'in their faces', just as we do. The best way to tread the fine line between interaction and over-stimulation is to respect your baby's signals.

Sometimes babies cry because they have simply 'had enough' and would just like to be left alone. Well, perhaps not exactly alone, but at least in relative peace and quiet. Babies may also find it more difficult to get to sleep when they are overtired, so it is important to be aware of your baby's signals and not extending her beyond her limits. (Each baby's signals are unique but signs of tiredness could include rubbing her eyes and nose as well as becoming increasingly disinterested in play, losing concentration, and 'grizzling'.)

'I discovered the secret is to watch Jacob's cues and put him to bed at the first sign of tiredness – before he gets overtired. I put him down and it's straight off to sleep 90 per cent of the

time. With our first baby, I missed these signals and when he stared to cry I would try to feed him, or rock him or walk the floor to settle him, and he got worse as he was overtired. Of course, there are times when Jacob falls asleep at the breast or while we are having a cuddle and that is really special for both of us.'

Bella, mother of two

'We went out to a barbecue last night, but it was right on Evie's bedtime. I took the pram thinking she could sleep in that, but no way! There were a few other babies there, so I didn't feel too bad about Evie's crying annoying anyone. I eventually rocked her to sleep in the pram after about 20 minutes of cry-ing/whingeing, but she woke up only fifteen minutes later, and would not be comforted. I finally admitted defeat, and we had to come home after only being out for two hours. I'm sure the other people were glad to see us take our crying baby and go! Evie cried all the way home, even though she normally loves the car. When I actually put her in her cot, it was almost a look of relief on her face, like "Finally these idiots have put me to bed to let me get some sleep!" She was asleep within seconds!'

Cassie, mother of a seven-month-old

50   *Babies may also find it more difficult to get to sleep when they are overtired, so it is important to be aware of your baby's tired signals and not extending her beyond her limits.*

'Our first child was born overseas – far away from family and friends (and the many stories/free advice). We only knew to parent the way that felt "right" to us. We always responded to Nikila's cues and often went days without hearing her cry. Our daughter travelled with us in a sling to many wonderful locations – it just never occurred to us that we would ever disturb anyone in a motel due to a crying baby, she was so content snuggled up close to us during the day and next to us in bed at night. It didn't take long for her to know that we would meet her needs and there was no reason to "scream" at us to do it. We wanted to do that, we wanted her to be happy, secure and loved.

'One night my very content daughter just let loose – it had been a busy day and because she spent most of the day in a sling next to me, you can easily forget how tired they may be. Her cry of exhaustion worried me. I had her close, she had been on the breast most of the day on and off, what else should I do? Taking a step back I realised that she needed to sleep, so I began our bedtime rhythm of bath, book, singing, boobie and bed... We were both asleep in no time. I reflected *the next day on how "disempowered" the previous night's episode made me feel – that sometimes even though we are doing everything that feels right there may be times when it also does not work. I learnt to respect my daughter's ability to communicate with me through the different cries she may use – I always responded.'*

Jane, mother of three

One trick at a time

It can be tempting to try every method you know to calm a crying baby, but if you have a sensitive little one who finds it difficult to move from one state (sleeping or waking, for instance) to another, or she is simply very tired, all your attempts to soothe her may actually be confusing and irritating rather than calming. Just do one calming thing at a time, quietly and gently, and watch her body language: is she relaxing or is she becoming even more excited or unhappy? If whatever you are doing is having the desired effect, don't stop and don't change tack. One trick at a time is enough.

'I found I got to know the difference between crying because of tiredness and other sorts of crying. If my babies wouldn't

settle quickly, I picked them up for a cuddle or a feed. It took a while to learn – I remember when my first daughter was seven weeks old she cried and fussed all morning. I tried feeding and comforting her, but nothing worked. Then I took her out to the first meeting of my new mothers' group. She continued to fuss and I didn't know what to do as she had never behaved like this before. She still wasn't really interested in feeding. Finally I put her in her pram in the corner of the room and within about a minute she was fast asleep!'

Sophie, mother of two

'Amazingly enough, the big change happened at eleven weeks when I was just getting to the point where I was going to die (I swear) if I didn't go to the toilet (I would put it off as long as possible so I wouldn't have to leave her crying). She was in her cot where I had been trying to settle her, so I closed the cot and literally sprinted to the bathroom. Within thirty seconds the crying had stopped and by the time I got back (maybe two minutes) she was sound asleep. I had been trying every single settling trick known and this was what worked!

'Today Caitlin is a pretty settled baby (and very smiley). Her cries are now easy to interpret and it is wonderful to know that whatever is wrong I can make it right for her – so far, touch wood.'

Rochelle, mother of a nine-month-old

Turn off the television

Although you might find it relaxing to veg out in front of television, a baby will find the constant noise and the flashing lights very stimulating. This sort of stimulus is not positive, however, even if it doesn't upset your baby, and it certainly won't be 'sleep-inducing'.

Often the tone of TV characters can be angry or scary, and your baby will sense these emotions. Even most children's programmes are too fast and 'flashy' for babies, and although babies and toddlers may be entertained they often need to release their pent-up energy afterwards and may do this by crying or becoming 'hyped-up'.

Most experts agree that you are certainly not depriving your infants if they never watch television. In fact, a 1999 policy statement by the American Academy of Paediatrics discouraged television-viewing for children under the age of two because 'research on early brain development shows that babies and toddlers have a critical need for direct interactions with parents and other significant caregivers for healthy brain growth and the development of appropriate social, emotional, and cognitive skills'. As with any aspect of child-rearing, you will have to use your own commonsense and judgement about whether you expose your baby to television and how you monitor this, but remember that mind-dulling habits are much harder to break if they are started early in life.

> **51**   Although babies and toddlers may be entertained by television, they often need to release their pent-up energy afterwards and may do this by crying or becoming 'hyped-up'.

Three in a bed

If you have a crying baby who has you jumping out of bed like a puppet on a string, taking your baby into your own bed could be the simplest solution all round. Chances are that you have probably already discovered how delicious it is to snuggle your cherub against your bare chest as you doze together after a night-time feed. On occasions when you have tried to stay awake waiting for your baby to finish a feed, then encountered wails of protest as you detached her from your warm body to move her back into her own bed, you may have surrendered and held your baby close a little longer. Perhaps you have woken hours later to discover you have all had a more peaceful sleep. But you dare not tell anybody for fear of criticism – you don't even know if it is a safe thing to do.

52 *If you have a crying baby who has you jumping out of bed like a puppet on a string, taking your baby into your own bed could be the simplest solution all round.*

Well, on the latter score your concerns should be eased when you hear that some of the lowest rates of **SIDS** are found in cultures where co-sleeping is predominant. There is also evidence that the risk of **SIDS** is significantly reduced when babies sleep in the same room as a responsible adult (not with siblings), and recent British guidelines advise keeping your baby in your room for the first six months. (Other tips for reducing the risk of **SIDS** include putting your baby to sleep on his back, avoiding overheating, and maintaining a smoke-free environment during pregnancy and the first year after birth. Co-sleeping parents (either parent) should also avoid alcohol and medications that may reduce awareness of their baby. Ensure the baby's head does not become covered by bedding and that she cannot sink into an overly soft mattress. You can find more detailed information on this topic in *Sleeping Like a Baby*.)

In addition to the **SIDS** factor, studies have confirmed that a mother who co-sleeps with her baby will instinctively move to avoid lying on her or impeding her breathing, even in deep sleep. Mother and baby also tend to get into the same sleep cycle, which means less crying for baby and more sleep for mother even if her baby does wake during the night. Babies who share a bed with their mothers arouse more frequently (though not necessarily waking) than babies who sleep alone. They also tended to sleep on their backs or sides and less often on their tummies (another SIDS risk factor).

If you do co-sleep with your baby, don't feel that you must go to bed early every night or should never allow her to sleep alone. There are many approaches to co-sleeping: you might put your baby in a cot until you're ready for bed or until she wakes for her first night feed, you could put her to sleep within easy reach in a baby hammock next to your bed, you might push her cot against your bed with one side down (make sure that neither the cot nor the bed can roll and leave a gap) so you can reach your baby easily, or you could use a cot that is especially designed to latch onto your bed such as the Arm's Reach Co-Sleeper, so baby is close but has her own space.

53 *Co-sleeping means that mother and baby tend to get into the same sleep cycle, which means less crying for baby and more sleep for mother even if her baby does wake during the night.*

If you sleep with your older baby and find she is waking and wanting to feed constantly at night, it may be because she can smell your milk. If you find this annoying and you don't think she is hungry or 'coming down with something' (increased feeding can be a signal that baby may be in the early stages of an illness), try turning her so she is facing away from you after she has been fed (or give her to your partner to cuddle). You can still cuddle and sleep together, but the breast will be less accessible and rocking her in your arms if you sense her waking may be enough to help her get back to sleep. Gradually she will not need to suckle in her sleep.

'Hugo was a most wakeful boy in the beginning – for the first nine months he woke every two hours in the night for a feed! The only way to survive with any vestige of sanity intact was simply to sleep with him so we had three in the bed. My husband sleeps soundly, even through the piercing cries of a hungry infant, so that is what we did. I would sleepily breastfeed whenever he wanted. I did notice, though, that while during the day breastfeeding would usually relax me and sometimes make me feel almost too soporific to read *A Suitable Boy*, at night it didn't seem to work quite so well. I'd often be wakeful after Hugo fell asleep. Perhaps that was because he would often need a nappy change as well – I don't remember.

'*Singing to him never helped at all (even though I sing OK, he would happily scream through the most venerable lullaby), and I was loath to try controlled crying as he was underweight and I figured if he wanted lots of feeds that was good both for his weight gain and for my supply.*'

Liz, mother of a toddler who now sleeps all night

'*I was the most relaxed with my first baby, as far as sleeping goes. I was a single parent and so slept with my daughter from birth. She breastfed completely on demand – I have absolutely no idea with what frequency. I was often asked by well-meaning, older- generation friends, "How often does she feed?" and I honestly would not have a clue. Whenever she wanted. Consequently she rarely cried. I had no hang-ups about this and we existed in our little world, seemingly communicating telepathically – happy mummy and happy child. She is now almost nine and the calmest, most beautiful child you could meet.*

'*My second daughter chose to sleep all night from birth! She also rarely cried and breastfed at will until she was two years and three months, which is when my third child took over the milking.*

'*My third child, a boy now fifteen months old, probably does a little crying at night just because I have so much less energy. I need the sleep! He is very happy but was waking several times through the night for feeds. I allowed this until he was a year old, but then I started to cuddle the baby when he woke, rather than feeding him because I reckoned it was comfort he was after, not food. He cried for hours the first time I tried it. The next night he slept right through – a fluke, of course. I have persisted in choosing not to feed him during the night and sometimes we get crying and others we don't. I do not feel he is being traumatised by this. His cries are of anger, not of pain or fear or even of sadness. 5.30 a.m. is the cut-off point between night and day, and he can have a breast then. If he is sick or teething I slacken off, and sometimes I'm just too exhausted to hold out. He rarely cries now, though, for more than a few minutes, and I have chosen not to feel guilty about my technique especially as he is such a happy and independent little kid who breastfeeds freely throughout the day.'*

Sally, mother of three

'I was living in America at the time I had my first child and had the Baby Wise style of parenting as my guide (this regimen has now been associated, by members of the American Academy of Paediatrics, with babies' failure to thrive). That's what the women around me were doing and I didn't think to do it another way. After a difficult and disempowering birth, I did schedule-feed my baby and do some controlled crying.

A few years later, as I found out more about demand feeding and having had a wonderful empowering VBAC (vaginal birth after caesarean) with my second child, I began to understand the psychological implications for my husband's and my actions. So I gave my first son, who was now three and a half, an opportunity to draw closer to me by sleeping with me, playing birth games, etc. He stayed in our room for almost a year before he felt like being in his own room again. It has been a wonderfully healing time for us and he can now express his emotions freely and is a more affectionate child. For me, it was a realisation that it wasn't too late to act on new information, clearer understanding and start making changes for the better.'

Erica, mother of two

Some other dos and don'ts

Leave her 'a little bit of Mum'

Co-sleeping may not appeal to you or your partner. Or sometimes you may just feel like a break: even the most devout proponents of 'attachment parenting' – a parenting style which involves keeping your baby close, 'baby-wearing' and co-sleeping – find there are times, in our culture at least, when they need to put their babies in a bed alone.

One way to help your baby sleep better by herself is to leave her a bit of yourself (well, a bit of your smell) behind. You can wrap a soft piece of clothing such as a nightie or t-shirt (recently used but not yet washed, so it smells like you) around your baby's mattress so she has access to your comforting scent as she sleeps. Or, if she is over a year old, simply give it to her to cuddle. This may come in particularly useful if you have to leave your baby with a sitter or she has to be fed by someone else: the sitter could wrap baby in her personalised cuddlie for her feed(s). It isn't exactly a substitute for you, but it will help reduce separation anxiety.

> **54** *You can wrap a soft piece of clothing such as a nightie or t-shirt (recently used but not yet washed, so it smells like you) around your baby's mattress so she has access to your comforting scent as she sleeps.*

Don't ever medicate your baby to make her sleep

No matter how desperate you are for sleep, please don't be tempted to dose your baby to get her to sleep. Even over-the-counter medicines may have sedative ingredients that could send her into a deep sleep from which she may not be able to arouse easily. Although this may be exactly the effect you are hoping for, it is potentially dangerous as your baby may not wake if she needs to. Recent research has, for example, linked use of the anti-histamine Phenergan with SIDS, especially for infants with colds, possibly because Phenergan (which has a sedative effect) decreases the swallowing and arousal reflexes that prevent choking. Phenergan should not be given to children under six months and some researchers recommend a minimum of two years.

In any case it is unwise to give a baby (or anybody else, for that matter) medicine if you aren't certain what the problem is. A crying baby is safer than a sedated baby. If you have any doubts about your baby's health, seek medical advice.

Do turn the clock to the wall

You just can't settle your crying baby. You check the clock: it's been two hours! You feel like crying too: you are exhausted now, so how are you going to feel in the morning? But worrying about those minutes – hours – ticking by is not going to help. In fact it's likely to make things worse as you become less and less relaxed and have less and less chance of getting back to sleep. Enter the downward spiral: you're anxious, your baby picks up on this and becomes more unsettled, you sleep less, and so on. The solution?

Simple: either remove the clock from the bedroom or turn it to face the wall at night.

'All three of my children needed to know I was close by at night. They were wakeful children and consequently slept less than the so-called "normal" baby. With all my children I tended to them quickly and offered the breast whenever they needed it. I have always felt instinctively that it was natural for my children to seek closeness and physical comfort from me – like a natural progression from the womb.

'I have used our rocking chair for many hours over the years to comfort and support our babies and children. Our children are welcomed into our bed whether it be as newborns, babies teething, toddlers needing company, our four-year-old with bad dreams, or just when they needed closeness.

'Babyhood is just a blink in a lifetime. I cherish these times, even when it is tiring and challenging. My most cherished moments are when I feed my babies in the quiet stillness of the night. I love the feeling of that tiny soft hand rubbing the bare skin of my back, or tiny fingers running through my hair. I would never have experienced these moments if I had not trusted my own instincts and stopped feeding through the night at the "recommended" time so my children would teach themselves to "sleep through".'

Donna, mother of three

Chapter six
Distractions and diversions

You may find you can head off tears at the proverbial pass, or avoid a full-blown crying episode, by introducing some fun and games or a change of scenery at a crucial moment. Many child-care experts put a lot of emphasis on 'settling' babies and/or on teaching them to sleep, but for most parents it doesn't actually matter whether their baby is asleep or awake so long as he isn't crying too much ('too much' is, of course, a relative term).

The fact is that babies don't just cry for physical reasons (hunger, tiredness, pain, discomfort) – like us, they have social needs and get bored if their lives are all 'work' and no play. If your baby is very young, you may dismiss boredom as a reason for crying. But any time you spend interacting with your baby during the early days may help avert tears (and extra effort on your part) in the months ahead, because it will help your baby develop skills that can pre-empt boredom and frustration.

Perhaps I should have said 'if Mum's day is all work and no play with baby', because play *is* a baby's work, and it is absolutely essential for their development. At the same time, if you simply do activities as though they are another worthy chore, your baby will sense your lack of enthusiasm. And if developmental advancement of your child is your main motivation, you are more likely to be overly serious and focused on your goals, rather than being in the present. Have fun by reconnecting with your own inner child and being spontaneous, and your baby will develop naturally at his own pace.

55 *Any time you spend interacting with your baby during the early days may help avert tears (and extra effort on your part) in the months ahead, because it will help him develop skills that can pre-empt boredom and frustration.*

'My husband has his own tricks for getting Evie to stop crying/calm down. He can always make her laugh, no matter how much she may have been crying five seconds before (he tickles her tummy with his beard!), and to get her sleepy he draws circles on the back of her neck – her head gets heavier and heavier!'

Cassie, mother of an eight-month-old

'We used to whisper right up close into our babies' ears. We'd say things like, "Are you a beautiful girl?", "Are you Daddy's

girl?" and other sweet nothings. It always worked and the girls
would settle immediately to hear what we had to say. Such
precious moments – it brings back sweet memories.'

Ruth, mother of two

Little distractions

At times when little ones are stressed or fractious, you may
need an instant distraction. Babies don't have the same
memory capacity that adults do (some adults, anyway –
maternal amnesia is a common side-effect of sleep deprivation!) So as they become demanding or yell because they
want something they can't have, it is easy to distract them
with an alternative.

By keeping a few simple props at hand, you can change
baby's mood (and your own) in moments. Here is a handy
arsenal of tear-busters.

> **56**   *Because babies don't have the same memory capac-*
> *ity that adults do, as they become demanding or yell because*
> *they want something they can't have, it is easy to distract them*
> *with an alternative.*

Play things

Bubbles

A bottle of bubble mix and some different-sized wands will provide instant amusement as you and baby try to catch shiny, shimmery bubbles. Blow a cascade of bubbles as a diversion when you change nappies and at bath-time, let them float in the wind outside, or blow some around baby on the carpet, where they will last a bit longer and give crawlers a chance to 'catch' them.

A bath

Get rid of that old association between baths and cleanliness: bath play is soothing and relaxing, and half an hour in the bath is certainly more pleasant than half an hour of grizzling. A bath can settle frayed nerves if you arrive home after a stressful trip to the supermarket, on a hot day as a 'cooler', or as bonding time between Dad and baby when Dad needs to relax or Mum needs a break. In the bath have fun with bubbles, splashy/squirty toys, and pouring in and out of empty household containers.

57 *Bath play is soothing and relaxing, and half an hour in the bath is certainly more pleasant than half an hour of grizzling.*

Balls

In the early weeks, a small colourful felt ball or a soft knitted ball makes for a lovely tactile experience. Later, a variety of balls large and small (but not small enough to fit into baby's mouth!) will facilitate all sorts of games and diversions.

Noise-makers

Make your own rattles by filling childproof containers with grains, lentils, rice, pasta or pebbles. Glue the lids on firmly and help baby shake them. Your crawling baby will have fun 'chasing' a noisemaker made from an empty (plastic) soft drink bottle containing some pretty pieces of tinsel or coloured paper and coloured beads or marbles, as well as noisy objects (make sure the lids are *very* secure).

Sew some little bells on a pair of baby's socks so they rattle when he kicks, or sew bells onto elastic to make jingly-jangly anklets.

Your older baby will love making his own 'music' by banging on pots and pans with spoons.

Scarves

Soft silky scarves provide both a visual and a tactile experience. Try swishing coloured scarves past your baby and/or stroking them across his bare tummy, and play 'peekaboo' as you pull a scarf backwards and forwards through a cardboard tube. Or make a magic scarf box: collect lots of old colourful scarves or squares of soft fabric, knot them together at one corner to make a long 'trail', and put this into an empty ice-cream container. Tape the last scarf inside the lid and make a neat hole in the bottom of the container (the bottom of the container will become the top of your magic box). Put the lid on the container, with the scarves squashed loosely inside, then pull the tip of the first scarf through the hole and show your little one how to pull it through to reveal the next brightly coloured scarf, and the next...

Mirrors

Hold your baby up to look at himself (and you) in the mirror. Hold one of his little hands or feet against the mirror and watch his fascination as you talk about who he can see there. My kids used to tell their baby brother that the little boy in the mirror was called Edward (not our baby's name) – I am sure this caused some awful confusion when he became a toddler and had to leave 'Edward' behind on the other side of the mirror.

Paper

Scrunch coloured paper into balls and roll them around the floor, or let baby scrunch a large sheet of wrapping paper himself. Little babies may enjoy kicking against scrunched-up paper at the foot of their basinet or cradle; give your bigger baby an old sock filled with scrunched-up paper or cellophane and then stitched or tied shut at the top. Supervise paper play strictly, as a wad of wet paper stuck in baby's mouth isn't fun, and avoid newsprint as it is messy and a bit toxic.

Cupboards

Make a low kitchen cupboard into a 'baby-safe' play zone: leave toys and/or safe household objects – plastic containers, utensils with smooth edges, empty packets – for baby to explore.

A basket of treasures

As your baby learns to sit, let him rummage (under strict supervision, of course) in a basket of humble household objects. Babies from six to nine months will explore objects with all of their senses – by sucking, smelling, grasping, mouthing, stroking, banging, rolling, tipping and examining them with great concentration. And as he is playing, your baby will also be learning to make decisions and choices, to concentrate and to store information.

What should you put in your baby's treasure basket? For starters, avoid plastic objects – they lack texture and smell. Instead, choose natural or textured materials such as large smooth shells, a plug on a chain, a soft brush, a small leather purse, a pinecone, a pretty rock, a woollen pompom or a felt ball, a small glass bottle (thick glass, please), a metal teaspoon, large wooden beads threaded on elastic, a natural sponge, beanbags made of various fabrics (such as velvet, corduroy, soft cotton) and filled with rice or popping corn. The possibilities are endless, but all the objects should be checked for sharp edges or for pieces that may break off easily. And you must always be with your baby when he uses the treasure basket, for safety's sake and so you can help if necessary. As an added precaution, check the contents of the basket before each play session.

Rotating toys

Thousands of dollars are spent on advertising 'essential' toys for babies. Bah, humbug! Don't be conned into spending a fortune – your baby doesn't need a squillion toys. Mostly he needs people to interact with and a few quality toys, along with interesting household objects and freedom to explore (this can't be stressed too much!)

One way to make the most use of toys is to rotate them. Choose a few different ones each day and put the others out of sight. Then, when boredom strikes, you can bring out a 'new' toy – this works for toddlers and older children too. Another suggestion is to check out your local toy library: this way, you get to see what your baby really enjoys before you go wasting big bucks on the latest fad, which mightn't amuse your baby at all, and you have a constant range of new and interesting toys.

> **58** *Choose a few different toys each day and put the others out of sight. Then, when boredom strikes, you can bring out a 'new' toy.*

Diversion therapy

Talk to your baby

Even the littlest baby will love a chat with people who love him, and he will feel your respect for him as a person – rather than a little object – if you speak intelligently to him right from the start. Tell him what is happening around him, and what you are doing as you change, dress and bath him. When he is a few months old, play little nursery games like 'This little piggy' or 'Round and round the garden'.

The more you talk to your baby and the more he is encouraged to respond, the sooner he will eventually learn to talk. And the less frustration you will both experience when he becomes a toddler: frustration is one of the major triggers for toddler crying – though we usually call it a tantrum at that stage! Provide a good model for your child by avoiding baby talk, and when he begins to say recognisable syllables (like 'ooh', 'aaah' or 'goo') or words, reinforce these by repeating them back to him and telling him how clever he is. Your pleasure and excitement will boost his efforts, whatever new skill he is practising.

As you talk, make eye contact with your little one and regularly give him the opportunity to have a conversation by pausing to let him babble back to you. Be theatrical with your gestures, laugh and giggle together, and reward your baby's efforts at communicating with smiles, cuddles and lots of attention.

Because so much of your baby's development will depend on his understanding of language, it is important to seek help from an appropriate health professional if you have any concerns about his hearing or if he seems unresponsive to your 'conversations' with him. If he has repeated ear infections, it is worth asking to see an allergy specialist, since allergies may cause a build-up of fluid in tiny ears.

59 *The more you talk to your baby and the more he is encouraged to respond, the sooner he will eventually learn to talk. And the less frustration you will both experience when he becomes a toddler.*

Read him a story

You might think that bedtime stories are for older children, but you can begin reading to your baby much sooner than that – even from birth. In fact, popular children's author and reading specialist Mem Fox claims that if all parents simply read three books a day to their babies from birth, this would eliminate illiteracy altogether.

At first it won't matter even if you read your baby the *Financial Review* – he will just love the sound of your voice. Soon, though, you will both discover that books provide a rich sharing experience: reading stories and looking at pictures exposes your baby to language and encourages conversation between you, and can be a lovely way for either parent to slow down during a busy day and connect with your child at *his* pace.

As you enjoy these special moments of closeness, your little one will develop his vocabulary and his ability to reason and make patterns of language and thought. He will make associations between pictures and stories and the real thing. Gradually he will learn how stories work and will begin making up his own stories and 'reading' to himself.

60 *At first it won't matter even if you read your baby the* Financial Review – *he will just love the sound of your voice.*

Tummy play

Some babies protest loudly when they are placed on their tummies, and many parents have become fearful of placing their babies on their tummies at all since **SIDS** research has shown that it is safer for babies to sleep on their backs. However, time spent lying on their tummies while they are awake is important in helping babies develop strong neck, shoulder, arm and torso muscles (rather like when, or if, we do push-ups). This strength will enable babies to crawl with ease and then to sit themselves up – and amuse themselves as they poke, taste and grab everything within reach! (These babies may even be safer when they do sleep, since they will have the strength to roll away if their breathing is obstructed.)

To encourage 'tummy time', place your baby on a firm, flat surface on his tummy with his arms forward – a rug on the floor is best, as a soft or padded surface makes it too hard for baby to move. To begin with, even on a firm surface, moving on their tummy is hard work for babies and they will tire quickly. The answer is short but frequent periods of play, allowing him to gradually build up his strength and learn to move more efficiently.

If your baby cries when you put him on his tummy, help him become more confident by playing some of these baby games:

- While you are lying on your back or reclining, lie your baby on your chest so that he will be encouraged to lift up and look at your face. Try gently rocking him from side to side as you hold him.
- Lie down on the floor facing your baby and talk or sing to him.
- Hold a rattle, a squeaky toy or a mirror in front of baby, for him to look at.
- Sit on the floor and hold your baby on his tummy across your lap or thighs. Gently stroke him rhythmically down his back, making circular motions between his shoulder-blades.

- Lie him on different textures: a (treated) lambskin or a 'feelie blanket' made of squares of contrasting fabrics such as soft velvet and corduroy, coarse hessian, shiny satin, and woollen, fleecy or fluffy fabrics. Curtain shops often sell sample squares of suitable fabrics in inexpensive bundles.
- Place a toy within baby's reach – perhaps a coloured ball or some shiny paper (under strict supervision).
- Swish your baby through the air to music, supporting him with your arms and hands under his body and chest.
- Lie baby across a beach ball or exercise ball, or a rolled-up sleeping-bag, and rock him gently to and fro and sideways: this will also stimulate his vestibular (balance) system and help him get used to being in different positions.
- Support baby on a rolled-up towel placed beneath his arms, so he can practise mini push-ups or play with a toy. (If you have the energy and resources, you can make the support out of foam rubber.)

Visual delights

Provide an array of visual experiences for your baby. Hang mobiles around the house and above the change-table, not only above his cot: he doesn't want to be stuck in a cot all day and, anyway, for the first couple of months his head will be turned to the side whether he is on his back or his stomach, so dingle-dangles directly overhead will be purely decorative. Remember, too, that your baby is mostly a horizontal being in the early months, so he won't have your vertical perspective – mobiles need to be three-dimensional or horizontal, otherwise he will simply view the dangly bits as a sharp edge.

Suspend mobiles out of reach, but where the wind will stir the hanging objects so they catch your baby's eye as you carry him past. For added fun and to help him learn cause and effect, show him how to blow the hanging objects or let him bat at them with his hands.

You don't have to spend a fortune buying mobiles, as they are easy and quick to make. Simply hang from a wire coathanger or a thin tree branch, some colourful shapes and objects: curls of coloured paper or aluminium foil, bottle-tops, coloured feathers and pieces of fabric; or angels, flowers and butterflies made from circles of coloured tissue-paper bound together with pipe cleaners.

The most natural mobiles of all are leafy branches, so lie your baby on a rug or in a pram beneath a tree where he can watch the interplay of light and shadow as the leaves move in the breeze (but don't leave him unattended). If you feel creative, try hanging some balloons from the tree branches for baby to watch as they blow around.

Other suitable amusements for 'horizontal' babies are objects strung on elastic across the cot or pram. You can also make these yourself by pegging interesting things to a length of elastic with clothes-pegs or those plastic clips that come with soft-toy chains; change the objects frequently to maintain interest. Or use a solidly made play gym that baby can pat and rattle as he lies on the floor. It is an important safety precaution to remove these toys from your baby's cot when he loses interest. Simplest of all, you can provide an endless procession of visual treats by taking your baby on outings where he can meet people and see new things (animals, flowers, water, vehicles). At home, keep him near you and the family, where the action is. Change the view by moving his cradle or cot around, but do keep it at a safe distance from curtain cords (which are strangulation hazards) and windows or windowsills (which may become escape avenues and/or falling hazards as he grows).

61 *Lie your baby on a rug or in a pram beneath a tree where he can watch the interplay of light and shadow as the leaves move in the breeze.*

Don't fence me in

The best place for your baby to play is on a clean floor where he can move and explore safely. In fact, baby equipment such as jumpers, walkers and playpens that confine your baby and restrict his movement are not only a waste of money but may even lead to more crying in the long run. There is, for instance, a significant fussy stage – commonly called 'the five-month blues', although it can happen earlier or later and often coincides with teething and separation anxiety – at which time babies are becoming increasingly aware of the world around them: they want what they see but they can't reach the object of their desire, so they cry! And they will cry louder and longer if they aren't mobile.

And while it may be tempting to prop your baby in a bouncer or stroller so he can watch the action, because he is quiet that way, or to place him in a baby walker to increase his view – and his reach, for which reason walkers are notoriously unsafe – you could be preventing him from going through other natural stages of development such as rolling over and crawling, then creeping on all fours. Not only is it neurologically desirable for babies to crawl before they can walk, but while crawling they explore the increasing range of textures and objects in their expanding environment and so develop their grasping, holding and letting-go skills, and stimulate hundreds of touch and position messages that flow to the brain. (If you do momentarily leave your baby in a bouncer or infant seat, please make sure to provide a safe environment away from pets or older, more mobile children who may bump the baby.)

Crawling is also important for babies to develop visual skills. For example, when they see a toy in the distance and move towards it, this facilitates focusing at varying distances. And, of course, because crawling and creeping are such vigorous exercise, your baby will be getting a workout – improving her breathing and co-ordination, and developing strength and muscle tone in her arms, hands, legs and feet – each time she does a lap of your living-room on all fours.

62 *Baby equipment such as jumpers, walkers and play-pens that confine your baby and restrict his movement are not only a waste of money but may even lead to more crying in the long run.*

Chapter seven
All the right moves

In your womb, your baby was gently rocked as you went about your daily activities, and even when you were resting the movement of the amniotic fluid rocked her little body. Becoming used to stillness is a new sensation for a newborn and well beyond that stage a gentle rocking motion will soothe your baby – and you.

Interestingly, the moves mothers make to calm a crying baby tend to duplicate the movement babies were accustomed to before they were born: when we rock babies in our arms, we typically do it at a speed which has the same rhythm as a pregnant woman's walk. And regardless of your own 'handedness' you will probably find that you instinctively hold your baby against your left side where she will find the sound of your heartbeat comforting (after all, this was the noise she heard constantly in the womb).

63 *Regardless of your own 'handedness' you will probably find that you instinctively hold your baby against your left side where she will find the sound of your heartbeat comforting.*

Walking the floor

Walking the floor – or the footpath – is not only a well-known baby soother, it is a sure-fire parent calmer too. Taking a long walk and breathing deeply as you do so oxygenates your body and releases endorphins (those feel-good hormones): as a result, your body chemistry changes and stress and anxiety melt away. So if the crying is getting you down and you feel like walking out, maybe you should – with your baby in tow or, even more effectively, in your arms! With luck, the sights and sounds and all that fresh air will mellow both baby and parent(s), or at least tire baby into a nice snooze so you can enjoy supper in peace. Often a late-evening walk will soothe baby to sleep. If you carry your baby in a sling, position her facing towards you, not outwards: your aim is to calm, not to stimulate her with sights and sounds at this time of day.

Walking or rocking your baby has other benefits too. The constant motion stimulates your baby's vestibular system (a part of her brain linked to the balance mechanisms of the inner ear), which enables her to integrate sensory messages and provides the foundations for language and other skills.

64 *If the crying is getting you down and you feel like walking out, maybe you should – with your baby in tow or, even more effectively, in your arms!*

'Take the baby for a walk outside. This will either (a) distract her, or (b) put her to sleep. And for you it will (a) distract you and (b) help you get some much-needed fresh air and exercise. Hopefully this will help you cope at night, when most of us can enlist the help of our partner.

'Most importantly, love her. Hold her while she cries, it feels so nice to be held while you're crying. She will feel your love, and it may take days, weeks or months, but the crying will pass and you will have loved her through it all.'

Gillian, mother of two

'I was probably never so fit as when our (now grown and calm) crying baby was little: I would "wear" her in a sling, with a poncho over both of us (she was a midwinter baby), and we would walk – and walk! Because she was our third child, I usually had her two older brothers in tow. It worked for all of us: she enjoyed the rhythm of the walk, I felt refreshed, and her brothers, like active puppies, were given a "run". This meant that they were more likely to be happy doing a quiet activity when I needed to walk the floor in the evening. Their father was working during the day, and because he was studying *was often at night classes when this baby was little, so he missed a lot of the crying. This meant I had to be in peak condition!'*

Molly, mother of five

There are lots of ways to walk and soothe – or sway and soothe: you will find yourself instinctively doing this in supermarket queues years after your crying baby has grown too big to fit on your hip! Whether you walk with your baby in a sling, or push her in a pram sometimes, whether you walk in the great outdoors or are confined inside because of bad weather, walking is a great soother. And when your legs are too tired to walk any further, you can still help your little one feel safe by holding her close where she will be comforted by the warmth of your body, your familiar smell, and the touch of your skin against hers.

Don't be put off venturing out by a concern that people will disapprove of you for not stopping to attend to your crying child: she will probably stop crying as soon as you get beyond your own gate anyway. If your baby does nod off in the pram or stroller, gently move her into bed when you get home, as an unattended pram isn't considered a safe sleeping environment. Do, though, remember to wait until her limbs are limp – a sign that she is deeply asleep – before you transfer her.

Walk before the wails

Don't wait for your baby to become inconsolable before you go walking. Research shows that carrying your baby may actually *prevent* crying. In one Canadian study where carrying was increased throughout the day (in addition to carrying during feeding and in response to crying) infants cried and fussed 43 per cent less overall and 51 per cent less during the evening. And, taking your baby outdoors during the day may help her tune into day and night rhythms earlier, which makes for better night-time sleeping.

So, as well as carrying your baby in a sling as you work, try a morning walk with your baby and your partner (and the poor neglected dog), or walk late in the afternoon – eat early and get your walking shoes on before the arsenic hour. To kill two birds with one stone, perhaps Dad could take baby for a walk in the evening to let Mum have some 'me' time – for a rest, a read, a relaxing bath, or whatever renews your energy and sense of self.

65 *Research shows that carrying your baby may actually prevent crying.*

A bumpy ride

Some parents swear by this as a soother, especially for 'colicky' or otherwise inconsolable babies. All it involves is pushing baby in her pram backwards and forwards over a bump – where levels change between rooms, say, or over a tiled floor. In fine weather, go outside and wheel her over gravel or any uneven surface.

A ride in the car – even late at night – is a last-resort baby calmer (bumpy doesn't matter here!) But don't do this if you are very upset or tired, as it is likely to affect your driving.

'Taking Stephanie for a walk in the night, either in my arms or in her pram, was very successful in settling her to sleep. Walking late at night was a safe option, as we lived on an isolated property. Living in hilly country we enjoyed a cooler climate, and I will always remember enjoying a walk along the track under the light of the stars, and the moon sometimes, with a cool or cold breeze on my face as I carried my baby wrapped in a shawl or pushed her in the pram. As well, I would sing to her quietly, "Twinkle, twinkle…" By the time I had walked a set distance and returned, she was well asleep and I was ready to sleep as well.

'Of course, some evenings a walk was not an option as it was not the weather for it or I did not have the energy in the

legs. On these occasions my good husband Phil would put a
on a CD of Stephanie's favourite music (Rolling Stones or Kate
Ceberano) and hold Stephanie for a couple of songs, dancing
slowly in the dark. The dancing routine had a great success
rate too.

'Stephanie would regularly save us the effort of the walk or
dancing by falling sound asleep suckling on the breast, which
was the easiest settling technique.'

Tania, mother of a four-year-old

66 *A bumpy ride can be a great soother. All it involves is*
pushing baby in her pram backwards and forwards over a bump
– where levels change between rooms, say, or over a tiled floor.

Experiment with carrying positions

With practice (and good luck), you will discover which carrying positions calm your baby most effectively.

Try an '**over-shoulder colic hold**' – carry your baby up
against your shoulder with her body pressed against yours.
She will be distracted by the view, and being in an upright
position will help if she has reflux or wind to burp up – but
don't try it in a dark business suit and remember to drape

a nappy over your shoulder to protect your clothing from milky spills.

Alternatively, try the '**colic carry**': lie baby face-down along one forearm (this may seem strange, but babies seem to enjoy facing the floor as you walk), with her legs straddling your arm and her cheek at your elbow, and support her with your other arm. Her head will be slightly higher than her body and the pressure of your forearm against her stomach will offer relief as you gently rock back and forth. A variation of this is the '**football hold**' – like the colic carry, only backwards: hold baby along your forearm with her chin supported in your hand and her legs straddling your elbow, then gently rub or pat her back, or rock her up and down. If she seems 'windy', carry her upright with her backbone against your body, pressing her knees gently against her stomach (put an arm under those tiny legs). When you're too tired to walk any more, try lying your baby tummy-down across your knees, perhaps with a well-wrapped, warm hot-water bottle or wheat bag on your lap.

Dads, as well as snuggling your baby against your bare chest with her ear over your heart, try snuggling your little one with her head nestled against your neck and the top of her head tucked under your chin. (Don't try to comfort your baby by holding her in a feeding position – this is a 'dry argument' for dads and will be frustrating for baby.) Sing as you walk: your baby will not only hear the song but also feel and be distracted by the vibrations from your larynx, even if you don't have the most soothing of voices. Chances are, your deep tones will lull her off to sleep!

> **67**   *Try the 'colic carry': lie baby face-down along one fore-arm (this may seem strange, but babies seem to enjoy facing the floor as you walk), with her legs straddling your arm and her cheek at your elbow, and support her with your other arm.*

Swings and roundabouts

You can both soothe your unhappy baby and provide extra vestibular stimulation (see 'Walking the floor' on page 185) by adding a few twists and turns to your carrying reper-toire. For instance, try shifting that wind and distracting baby by holding her in your arms and bending both your knees as you alternately lower and lift her up to provide an 'up and down' motion (this is more like the motion she experienced in the womb than a sideways rocking motion). Alternatively, walk around in circles or up and down stairs, or slowly swivel on an office chair as you hold your baby –

the changing view may distract her as the motion soothes. If you are out walking, stop in the park and ride on the swings with baby in your arms or a sling; if your arms are tired or you need some time out, an infant swing may also be soothing.

'My first three months with my baby son were a nightmare. He cried a lot in hospital post the birth, but we figured that was to do with a traumatic birth – he was distressed and had the ventouse (suction) delivery, so had a rather sore head. The crying got worse when we got home. I reckon I read every book and clutched at any idea that might work to settle him. We would have days where between 12 noon and midnight he would scream except when feeding. We tried wind drops, elevating the head of his cot, Mylanta after feeds, aromatherapy oils, massage, warm baths, sleep CDs, changing my diet (breastfed baby), rocking him, baby hammocks, leaving him to cry – all to no avail. Eventually I contacted our local parenting help organisation, who sent someone to our house: her best suggestion was for us to hire a nanny so we could get a break – as if we could afford that! We did eventually buy a battery-operated swing which was fantastic in calming him and even sent him off to sleep sometimes.'

Rachel, mother of a five- month-old

68   *Walk around in circles or up and down stairs, or slowly swivel on an office chair as you hold your baby – the changing view may distract her as the motion soothes.*

On your bike!

Another trick, if foul weather prevents you from pounding the footpaths and a crying baby is leaving you little time to exercise, is to put baby into her sling and get pedalling – on your exercise bike. You won't have to worry about finding a helmet for her, and you will be in peak condition by the time the weather improves. Then, when your cherub is old enough, you can buy her a helmet and an infant seat, and take her for a ride on a real bike.

'My sure-fire baby calmer is my exercise ball – I used it to keep fit during pregnancy and now it works wonders to calm my eight-week-old baby when he cries. One advantage of this is that I don't have to be on my feet (a plus when you are ready to drop from exhaustion!) We just put on some soft music and gently bounce, rock and swivel until sleep descends. Another plus is that my tummy muscles are getting a gentle workout at the same time! Bub just loves the bouncing action – we use it for play, too.'

Janet, mother of one

Rock-a-bye baby

For parents of a crying baby (in fact, for parents of any baby) a rocking chair has to be high on your list of nursery furniture – up there with the car capsule and a baby sling. Rocking can be either stimulating or soothing to a baby, depending on her mood at the time. So whether she is crying from boredom or tension, snuggling together in a rocking chair will have a calming effect (on both of you). And this is one nursery item that won't be outgrown: you can rock and sing , rock and read together, or simply rock, whenever you need to dissipate tension – with or without your baby!

A rocking cradle has the same soporific effect as a rocking chair. If you choose to use one, though, make certain it has a locking mechanism and use this vigilantly when you are not watching your baby as otherwise she may rock herself into a corner (a suffocation risk). A safer and equally effective way to lull your baby to sleep is a special-purpose baby hammock (see the Resources section): this contains baby much as she was confined in utero, and as she moves and arouses her own movements gently start the hammock rocking.

69   *Rocking can be either stimulating or soothing to a baby, depending on her mood at the time. So whether she is crying from boredom or tension, snuggling together in a rocking chair will have a calming effect (on both of you).*

Keep the beat

In traditional cultures, the comforting beat babies became used to in the womb is continued after birth, in daily life: as they are carried on their mothers' backs, these babies are exposed to the beat of grinding, milling and sweeping, and to live music such as drumming and singing. In 'advanced' societies such as ours, we are much less likely to expose our babies to this pulsating heartbeat of life. Yet, according to early childhood educator and music specialist Tessa Grigg, keeping the beat not only comforts children but is a prerequisite for the development of physical skills.

You can comfort and help your baby get rhythm by gently patting her body in time to music and playing maracas, rhythm sticks or bells as you sing or play music. Soon your baby will be able to use the noise-makers herself (you can buy bells on elastic that fit onto children's wrists, or sew some bells onto elastic yourself). Provide live music too, by singing to your baby – make up words if you can't remember them, and include your baby's name in the songs you sing. Hold her on your knee, facing you, and bounce her gently up and down in time to your singing – try this to old-fashioned songs like 'Skip to my Lou' or 'The Grand Old Duke of York' (raise your knees at 'and when they were up, they were up', and lower your knees for 'and when they were down, they were down').

70 *Share the rhythm. Hold her on your knee, facing you, and bounce her gently up and down in time to your singing.*

Sing me a song

Babies would much rather listen to the voices of people they know and love, even if they aren't in perfect harmony. So shed your inhibitions, and those awful memories of being put at the back of the school choir (for volume!), and sing to your baby.

Just for inspiration, here are some rhymes and songs with actions, to help you entertain and connect with your little one by the most soothing sound of all – your voice.

'Head and Shoulders, Knees and Toes'

You will be able to keep up with the playgroup mums, as well as help your bub learn her body parts, if you learn this one! It is also a great singing game if you need to involve a toddler as you sing to your baby.

Use your baby's hands to touch the different parts of her body as you chant them. If she's lying down rather than sitting up and the knees and toes may be a bit hard to reach, either touch them for her or just pat her arms in the general direction. Once she is old enough to sit securely you will probably be able to help her reach these parts.

Head and shoulders, knees and toes, knees and toes.
Head and shoulders, knees and toes, knees and toes,
And eyes and ears and mouth and nose,
Head and shoulders, knees and toes, knees and toes.

'My Bonnie Lies Over the Ocean'

My bonnie [or baby's name] lies over the ocean,
(rock baby gently to the left)
My bonnie lies over the sea,
(rock baby to the right)
My bonnie lies over the ocean.

(lean baby backwards)
Oh, bring back my bonnie to me.
(snuggle baby to your chest)

Bring back, bring back,
Oh, bring back my bonnie to me, to me.
Bring back, bring back,
(rock baby backwards and forwards)
Oh, bring back my bonnie to me.
(snuggle baby to your chest and end with a big cuddle)

'Down by the Station'

This is a song with a beat you can exaggerate: the actions are fun, either as you bounce baby on your knee, or on mornings when you are sitting up in bed with baby. Sit her on your tummy, facing you and with her back resting against your bent knees. Hold her hands in yours and move her arms so they cross over her chest in time to the beat as you sing.

Down by the station, early in the morning,
See the little puff-a-billies standing in a row.
See the engine driver, pull the little handle,

(move baby's arms up in the air and down together),
Toot, toot, puff, puff, off we go!
(give her a raspberry on the neck or tummy)

Soothing sounds

All over the world, throughout history, mothers have instinctively soothed crying or unsettled babies by singing lullabies.
Many of these songs are handed down from generation to
generation, and usually they have repetitive, calming tones
that recall the rhythm of the mother's heartbeat and the
'womb music' heard before birth: the hum of blood flowing
through your veins, the whoosh-whoosh of blood pumping
through your arteries and the placenta, the gurgling of your
digestive system, and the gentle sea-like noises of air flowing in and out of your lungs as you breathe.

As well as lullabies, there is a whole range of music
styles and rhythmic beats which will have varying effects
on your baby (and you) – from diverting and stimulating
her, and making her feel happy, to helping her relax. The
health benefits of singing and playing music to babies,
especially premature infants, are now recognised. According to one study at the University of California Medical
Centre, premature babies in intensive care who were

exposed to classical music were calmer, used oxygen more efficiently, gained weight faster and their head circumference (which indicates brain size) increased. Another study showed that playing 60-minute tapes of lullabies and children's songs reduced the hospital stays of premature and low-birth-weight babies by an average of five days. Music has also been shown to have pain-relieving benefits for babies. So if you have a sick or premature, crying baby, you can use music to enhance bonding and actively assist healing and growth. And, of course, if music has such therapeutic benefits for babies with special needs it is undoubtedly beneficial for all babies.

71 Many lullabies are songs handed down from generation to generation, and usually they have repetitive, calming tones that recall the rhythm of the mother's heartbeat and the 'womb music' heard before birth.

'Sam was in the Special Care Unit for ten days before coming home. It was very scary for my husband and I as we had not had the opportunity to spend time with him in hospital. As marvellous as the staff were, the one-hour crash course in parenting prior to him leaving the hospital only got us as far as the first day.

'With the help of friends, family and the parent help lines, we eventually muddled our way through the first week. In hospital we noticed they played music to the babies pretty much 24 hours a day. After quite a few sleepless nights, we decided that music in his room was a good idea. Kenny G, Richard Clayderman and the 'Music for Dreaming' CD worked really well. Previously Sam would fuss for half an hour before going off to sleep, but by putting on this music as we put him in his basinet, now he sometimes goes to sleep without a peep.'

Julie, mother of a six-week-old

'I have a photograph taken of me with my son Christopher, who as a premmie caesar baby developed complications shortly after birth and was placed in a humidicrib, on an assisted-breathing table for four days. The photograph (I don't know who took it) is a silhouette of me standing looking at my son who was so desperately ill, and willing him on by telling him all the things we would miss out on if he did not survive. I stayed glued to the table, with just short snatches away to visit my wife who was also struggling with her post-operative care. As she could not be there, I felt I had to convince my son to fight for a future that included a very special bond between mother and son.

'I don't recall all of the hours or the ups-and-downs during that period, but I do vividly recall the moment Christopher

decided to live. Clarity so strong that to this day I can still remember what it was I was saying.

'When I was a child we learnt a song at school that became my mother's favourite whenever we were travelling in the car. I had not even remembered it prior to this time, but it suddenly came into my head and I was hesitantly singing it in a soft "only for him" voice. Christopher's chest was dragging in every breath through what can only be described as sandpaper, and the rattling noise at every intake was laboured and angry. As I finished the words I said, "That was Grandma's favourite song and if you stick around I will sing it to you often." With that, the taut expression on his face smoothed and his chest just sighed in relief. A small smile played over his face in approval and even the monitors that recorded his precarious state seemed to quieten for an instant.

'Now he is seven and in times of particular stress I will sing this song with him. It still works like magic. I wonder how old he will be before I am banned from singing:

Hippity Hoppity,

Flippity, Floppity,

Through the green bushes and over the hills.

Out of the burrows and over the furrows,

Those dear little bunnies can never keep still.

If I show you a juicy green lettuce,

Or a tender young carrot to munch,
Won't you play with me just for a minute,
Just for one minute and nibble some lunch?
Hippity Hoppity,
Flippity, Floppity,
Through the green bushes and over the hills.
Out of the burrows and over the furrows,
Those dear little bunnies can never keep still.'

Peter, father of two

As well as having therapeutic benefits, those lilting lulla-bies with which you soothe the sobs (even if your baby is your only appreciative audience) could also be having remarkable effects on your child's development. It seems that if you want to raise a happier, brighter child, the secret is to surround her with music – even before birth: prena-tal exposure to music has been credited with enhancing visual tracking and eye–hand co-ordination, and creating memories that will soothe your baby if you play her the same tunes after birth. If you think you have missed the boat here, take heart. Think back to style(s) of music you listened to while you were pregnant, and chances are that this will be the music that calms your baby now, even if she is already a few months old. On the other hand, if by sheer brilliance you are reading this while you are pregnant, now is the time to start playing your baby's special relaxing music so you can use it to calm her (and you) later.

An English study has shown that babies can recognise music they had been played while in the womb, up to a year after birth. It doesn't seem to matter, either, if the music you exposed your baby to in the womb wasn't gentle classical music. The parents in that study represented a wide variety of economic and social backgrounds, and the babies were introduced to many different types of music during their first year – including popular, classical and reggae – and their preferences ranged accordingly. It is generally agreed that a variety of music can have beneficial effects. Music therapist Don Campbell, famous for his research and books about 'the Mozart Effect', advises parents that:

> 'from the very beginning, you can make use of happy nursery songs, rhythmic rocking, lively dances bounced on the knee, and quiet sessions with classical recordings to bring harmony, mental stimulation and joy into your baby's life. Western classical music, along with chants, nursery rhymes, and songs of early childhood, contains all the rhythms and patterns of language, whether that language is English

or Swahili. Thus, teaching your infant to appreciate music helps prepare his brain for mastering language's complex structure.'

Using music to soothe or interact with your baby can also help the day go more smoothly by helping her move gently from one activity to another or to endure some of the more mundane aspects of her day (and yours). Singing songs now, as you bath her, wash her hair, travel in the car or prepare her for bed, will enable you to use the same rituals to melt resistance when she reaches the more wilful toddler stage.

'Andre loves me singing "Old MacDonald Had a Farm". So far, for the last month and a half, this has worked wonders for calming him down.

   'The first couple of months, he loved to fall asleep to Sting's Nothing Like the Sun *CD and my mum singing to him.'*

Claudette, mother of a five-month-old

'For the first child, we finally found she fell asleep to a Sheryl Crow CD by the middle of the second track. For the second child, she just seemed to be plain-old thirsty (must've been that hot weather).'

Melissa, mother of two

'For us the tape in the car saved many trips. Very quickly Harry knew which tapes were his favourites. At a young age (three months), if I put a tape on that he did not like he would cry and the instant I changed it to something he liked all would be quiet. Now at twenty-two months I can't even get the car out of the garage without a little voice from the back seat saying, "Music, music," and then he says, "It's coming!"'

Tessa, mother of one

'My mum sings to Evie and rocks her when she gets a bit grizzly, and always manages to calm her down, but it doesn't work when I try it (my singing voice isn't that bad!) If Evie and I are having a bad day, I usually take her up to my mum's house and let Nana take over for a bit!'

Cassie, mother of one

Calming music

If your aim is to lull your baby to sleep, probably the most effective music to play is gentle classical with a steady tempo and a slow rise and fall, such as Mozart or Vivaldi. Many experts recommend the 'Baby Bs' – Bach, Beethoven and Brahms – whose compositions seem to calm babies and parents alike. Avoid hard rock and electronic music, as these may irritate your baby's nervous system. Instead, expose your baby to the rich pure sounds of traditional instruments.

> **72** *Probably the most effective music to play is gentle clas-sical with a steady tempo and a slow rise and fall, such as Mozart or Vivaldi. Many experts recommend the 'Baby Bs' – Bach, Beethoven and Brahms – whose compositions seem to calm babies and parents alike.*

Studies show that babies just 24 hours old can recognise their mother's voice, so if you are going to use lullabies for calming purposes it is best to gently hum or sing yourself, rather than playing the recorded voice of a stranger. You can sing unaccompanied, or to an instrumental tape. Of course, if you are talented enough to play an instrument your baby can have it all – live music and a familiar parent's voice!

'My son will stop crying immediately to the first strains of "The Lion Sleeps Tonight", doesn't matter what version! I like the song and so would sing it to him as part of my normal reper-toire when I was settling him (I have sung and had lessons for years, so it's almost second nature for me to sing him to sleep). The song also helps me to settle down, as the words are like a lullaby".

'Anyway, I noticed he became more settled to this song, so I found a version of it on The Lion King CD. Even if he's screaming from wind he will just stop and usually go to sleep after I play it through once or twice. I never played it during the pregnancy, so I can't work out why he likes it so much. All I can say is the neighbours must be getting mighty sick of it!

'The Music for Dreaming CD has also worked well in the evening, but for settling during the day Dylan likes something with a beat, like U2 or REM. I think he likes the rhythm they have, sort of like patting baby's back.'

Miriam, mother of a nine-week-old

'When Jackson is crying, we play his "baby" music (Music for Dreaming). At first we put it on with the volume turned up loud to match the volume of his cries, then as he stops to listen we reduce the volume – it works every time. We also put this music on playing continuously at night when we put him to bed and we hear him "talking" to the music if he wakes during the night.'

Oscar, father of a four-month-old

73 Studies show that babies just 24 hours old can recognise their mother's voice, so if you are going to use lullabies for calming purposes it is best to gently hum or sing yourself, rather than playing the recorded voice of a stranger.

If you want to use music as a sleep cue, or to wean your baby off the breast at night-time, play the same music each night so that it becomes the go-to-sleep music, then gradually replace the breastfeed with that music. If you have a baby who is waking often during the night, you may find a continuous-playing tape recorder with the go-to-sleep music on low helps your baby to settle and sleep as she hears her familiar tunes. In any event, since you can bet your boots that baby will be almost asleep just as a piece of music ends and will, of course, wake when the music stops or changes tracks, look for a tape or CD that plays continuous music, such as *Music for Dreaming* (see the Resources section). Almost any song sung quietly and lovingly can help induce sleep, but here are some traditional lullabies to try:

'Brahms Lullaby'
   Lullaby, and goodnight –
   go to sleep little baby,
   Close your eyes now
   sweetly rest.
   May your slumbers be blessed.
   Close your eyes now
   sweetly rest.
   May your slumbers be blessed.

'Hush Little Baby'

> Hush little baby, don't say a word,
> Papa's gonna buy you a mocking-bird.
> And if that mocking bird won't sing,
> Papa's gonna buy you a diamond ring.
> If that diamond ring turns to brass,
> Papa's gonna buy you a looking-glass.
> If that looking glass gets broke,
> Papa's gonna buy you a billy goat.
> If that billy goat don't pull,
> Papa's gonna buy you a cart and bull.
> And if that cart and bull turn over,
> Papa's gonna buy you a dog named Rover.
> If that dog named Rover don't bark,
> Papa's gonna buy you a horse and cart.
> If that horse and cart fall down…
> You'll still be the prettiest little baby in town!

White noise

While some babies are instantly spooked by the whirr of a vacuum-cleaner (a perfectly legitimate excuse to avoid housework), others seem to be hushed by 'white noise' such as this – the buzz of a radio set between stations, or a fan or air-conditioner (but don't ever leave a fan where a baby could reach it). The theory behind using white noise to calm babies seems to be that these sounds will actually help her tune out to other stimuli that may be overwhelming. Give it a try (wear your baby in a sling while you vacuum, for double brownie points!) – it might just work.

Other non-musical sounds that may help calm a crying baby include a ticking clock or an electric shaver (with the cap on) wrapped in a cloth and placed next to baby, or a dishwasher or washing machine (you really can't avoid all housework!) If you want to spend money, you might like to try a tape of ocean sounds or womb sounds.

> **74** *Non-musical sounds that may help calm a crying baby include a ticking clock or an electric shaver (with the cap on) wrapped in a cloth and placed next to baby, or a dishwasher or washing machine (you really can't avoid all housework!).*

Baby dancing

To comfort your baby, combine the sound of your voice (as you hum or sing to the music), the security of your arms (as you hold your little partner), and movement (as you dance together). Try a 'colic waltz', which continues the tempo your baby was familiar with in the womb – the natural rhythm of your resting heartbeat is a three–four beat. Find some old waltz tunes and play them as you dance with your baby in your arms: *one* (big step), two three (shorter steps); o*ne*, two three; o*ne*, two three…

Of course, you can increase your repertoire. Your baby will grow to love whatever tunes convey happy feelings to you both (see 'Soothing sounds' on page 200), and yes, you can add fancy steps of your own. Why not try a few twirls? Just not on a full stomach!

75 *Try a 'colic waltz', which continues the tempo your baby was familiar with in the womb – the natural rhythm of your resting heartbeat is a ¾ beat.*

Chapter eight
Tender touch

If you have a baby who cries excessively, is unresponsive or has special needs, it is often more difficult to feel connected with him, especially if either or both of you feel stressed much of the time. Regardless of your baby's temperament or needs, it is important to include positive interactions that go beyond basic care and coping, but this is absolutely vital when you are experiencing the challenges and stress of a crying baby. Infant massage is a tender way to enhance the relationship between Mum or Dad and baby by incorporating all the important elements of parent–child bonding such as skin, eye and voice contact.

> 'Our special family friend Jacqueline gently bathed, then massaged, our second daughter with the love and gentleness of a "wise woman". We learnt from it, just watching. We then imitated the soothing strokes and it worked – it really worked, and we all felt great.'
>
> **Jane, mother of three**

Massaging your infant is not only good for your relationship. Your loving touch has profound effects on his development, especially his immature nervous system (which has been cited as a possible cause for unexplained crying). Massage can stimulate nerves in the brain which facilitate food absorption, resulting in faster weight gain: a University of Miami study found that premature babies who were massaged three times a day for fifteen minutes each time, over a ten-day period, gained 47 per cent more weight and were discharged from hospital six days earlier than babies who were touched or cuddled only during feeds and nappy changes. Similar results have been obtained in studies of stressed and failing-to-thrive cocaine-exposed babies who were massaged. The babies in these studies didn't actually eat more, they simply absorbed food more efficiently; follow-up studies showed that these benefits had lasting effects.

76 *Your loving touch has profound effects on your baby's development, especially his immature nervous system (which has been cited as a possible cause for unexplained crying).*

Massage can also help relieve colic and constipation, encourages babies to become more alert and responsive, and is a wonderful tool for calming babies and promoting sound sleep. Another study from Miami University showed that infants and toddlers who were massaged daily by their parents for one month, for fifteen minutes prior to bedtime, fell asleep more easily by the end of the study.

Massage is a beautiful way to keep in touch as your baby grows, and provides an opportunity for him to develop body awareness, especially if you talk to him about his 'cute little fingers and wriggly toes' or tell him, 'You are growing so long' as you stroke along his back. And while your baby enjoys receiving a massage, you will also enjoy giving it – who can resist that delicious baby-fine skin?

77 *Infants and toddlers who were massaged daily by their parents for one month, for fifteen minutes prior to bedtime, fell asleep more easily by the end of the study.*

Be prepared

It will be beneficial for you, your partner and your baby to attend a series of infant-massage classes. If this isn't practical, you can order my *Gentle Beginnings* baby massage DVD (see Resources).

Remember to keep your nails clipped and use hand lotion regularly to soften any rough patches on your palms (Dads too). Always warm your hands before giving a massage, by rubbing them together or holding them under warm water (dry them thoroughly).

'I have massaged my daughter since she was two days old. Mia is now three and massage continues to be an important part of the way we bond. Though I have heard stories about parents being able to use massage to stop their child from crying, I never found this to be the case with Mia. I believe, however, that Mia was able to be soothed by me in times of stress because of the physical and emotional connection that we share. The quality time spent during massage certainly played a major role in developing this closeness.

'My second child, Kai, experienced a problem with constipation at around three months of age. He woke early in the morning crying with pain. I began massaging his tummy calmly and he stopped crying almost immediately. Ten minutes after his massage there was most certainly an urgent need for a nappy change. I felt so confident in my role as a parent, knowing that when he was in pain and crying I was able to help by doing something constructive. I think this confidence also helped my child to relax as opposed to picking up on tension.

'*Massage plays an important role in our family, though Kai doesn't know it yet, at only five months. Mia not only receives massage but also offers massage to me, her dad, and Kai; and as she sees me and her father exchange shoulder rubs she is learning that physical contact within a family is okay and that you can show affection and receive comfort from your family when you need support or just need to feel loved.*'

Heidi, mother of two

Create a calm space

Establish an environment with a pleasant atmosphere so your baby will associate the smells, sights and sounds of this special place with the soothing experience of being massaged: warm the room, play soft classical music, and avoid harsh lighting – open the curtains and bathe the room in natural light, but make sure bright sun is not shining directly into your baby's eyes. Take the phone off the hook, hang a 'Do Not Disturb' sign on the front door and have everything at hand, including nappies and a special soft blanket, towel or lambskin to lie baby on. Babies find it difficult to regulate their own body temperature and may feel cool as they relax, so have a soft blanket within reach to cover exposed parts as you massage. Your baby will soon come to associate his special 'massage place' and things like his towel or blanket as cues that your precious, sharing time together is imminent.

Just as you create a familiar environment for massages, try to find a time of day that suits you both and encourage your baby to relax into a gentle daily rhythm by massaging him at this time each day. Young babies may find it too stimulating to incorporate a bath and massage one after the other, but as baby grows it may suit to massage him after his bath, for instance, or between feeds when he is in a quiet state of alertness.

78 *When you first massage your baby, do so while he is calm and choose a time of day when he will associate the experience with a calm and happy feeling. In this way, you'll be able to use massage to soothe him later on, as he grows.*

The good oil

Studies indicate that babies prefer to be massaged with oil: they show fewer stress behaviours like grimacing and clenched fists, and lower cortisol (stress hormone) levels when they are massaged with oiled rather than dry hands.

A cold-pressed vegetable oil, such as olive or jojoba oil, will nourish the skin, feels pleasant and won't hurt baby if he sucks his hand. Don't use a mineral-based oil: this may clog tiny pores and is absorbed through the skin and when later excreted by baby may take some vitamins with it. Some babies may be sensitive to particular oils, or to additives such as preservatives and chemicals, so read labels carefully to check for ingredients. If you have any concerns about your baby's sensitivity, test by applying a little oil on a small patch of skin beneath your baby's forearm and leaving it overnight: if there is any reddening or a rash, don't use this oil. And, for safety's sake, do remember that oily babies are slippery!

Use oil sparingly. Don't pour oil directly onto your baby's skin: instead, warm the oil and pour a little into your own hands to check the temperature first, and allow it to warm or cool to your body temperature before massaging.

79 *Babies show fewer stress behaviours like grimacing and clenched fists, and lower cortisol (stress hormone) levels when they are massaged with oiled rather than dry hands.*

Soothing scents

Aromatherapy is the practice of healing through scent: it uses a range of essential oils (extracted from various plants), each of which has its own scent, colour and healing properties. Lavender and chamomile, for instance, are well known for their calming qualities.

Pure essential oils, or oils incorporated in products such as bath oil, can have calming effects when used for massage or added to your baby's bath. Products containing essential oils are not, however, recommended for babies under three months old. Seek advice from a natural health practitioner or a qualified aromatherapist before you use essential oils or related products, to make sure they are appropriate for use with babies. And as with any oil applied for massage, always check labels and test a sample of any product before you use it on your baby. Essential oils shouldn't be applied directly to the skin. If using one for baby massage, first dilute it with a carrier oil such as grape-seed or sweet almond oil.

For colicky babies, try a gentle tummy massage with a few drops of chamomile oil mixed with a carrier oil. And remember that it's not just baby who will benefit from aromatherapy: try dabbing a few drops of lavender oil on your own wrist if you are feeling tense, or add a few drops in water to an oil burner and create a calm environment for the entire family.

80   For colicky babies, try a gentle tummy massage with a few drops of chamomile oil mixed with a carrier oil.

Tune in to your baby

Is the time right to give your crying baby a massage? Learning to read your baby's cues is much more important than which massage technique you use. By respecting your baby's attempts to communicate, you are teaching him in the gentlest possible way that he is safe, that his body belongs to him, that his feelings are important, that he has a right to refuse unwanted touching.

Before you begin to massage your baby, connect with him and ask, 'Would you like a massage?' or tell him gently, 'We are going to have a massage now. I am going to pick up your tiny foot and stroke it,' or, 'I am going to rub your silky little head.' Watch him and wait for a response.

As you massage, make eye contact with your baby and watch his facial expressions. Talk to him and wait for him to 'reply'. Tune in to his responses and try to understand what he is communicating: is he saying, 'Yes, I'm enjoying this,' or, 'I've had enough, please stop'? Is he relaxing, or does he tense up when you touch particular parts of his body? Depending on his response, you may need to stop massaging and give him a cuddle, or gently get him used to experiencing touch if he expresses sensitivity in certain areas.

81 *Learning to read your baby's cues is much more important than which massage technique you use.*

Sometimes your baby's response may mean abandoning the massage until another time. Your baby's likes and dislikes will be unique to him, just as they are with adults. If he seems to want to change position, or becomes agitated and doesn't seem to want a full massage, just go with the flow. You will soon learn which strokes he prefers, and as a result you will develop a style of massage you both enjoy. This can change from day to day, depending on your baby's needs and stage of development. Some babies, for instance, don't like being touched on the head at first, perhaps because of pressure to this area during the birth. Others can't tolerate too much stimulation, so a short massage will be enough initially, after which you can gradually increase the time and/or gently accustom your baby to massage in sensitive areas as his 'touch tolerance' increases.

Even a short massage of your baby's feet or hands, or face and ears, or a gentle back rub, will make a difference to his wellbeing, as there is a cluster of reflexology and acupuncture points in feet, hands and ears. The ancient healing art of reflexology was first practiced by the early Indians, Chinese and Egyptians: they observed that congestion or tension in any part of the foot mirrors congestion or tension in a corresponding part of the body. Thus, when you treat the big toes there is a related effect in the head, and treating the whole foot can have a relaxing and healing effect on the whole body. I was first taught infant massage by a Sikh woman who showed me how to massage a reflexology point on the back of my baby's heel which, if massaged daily for the first three years of her life, would help her develop a photographic memory – she certainly remembers when it's my turn to buy the petrol! Acupressure, a traditional Chinese practice, works on the theory that a series of channels – referred to as meridians, and a separate network from the nervous, blood and lymphatic systems – carry *chi* (energy) throughout the body. It is believed that pressure at points along the meridians will unblock, calm or strengthen the flow of energy around the body. One pressure point to try: massaging the soft part of the hand between the thumb and forefinger is said to help teething.

If your baby resists massage, or if massage isn't appropriate (perhaps he has fever, is unwell or has just been immunised), offer him close body contact in other ways: hold him against your bare chest, have a bath with your baby or hold your hand against his bare back under his clothing (nighties offer more opportunities for skin contact with little babies than gro-suits).

'Hey, what about us?'

Children instinctively enjoy giving, as well as receiving, massage. If you have other children, rather than waiting for them to be quiet or otherwise occupied, or having them feel left out, include them at massage times: if you have a high-needs baby who requires a lot of your time, he will need positive interactions with his (possibly resentful) older siblings. Let a toddler help by stroking baby's hand or foot, or allow a much older sibling to do some massaging, and watch the interaction. Sharing massage is a lovely way to encourage a connection between an older child and a new baby.

'I went to infant massage classes with my first child, Ruby, when she was about three months old. Right from the first

lesson, the way she responded to my touch was magical. She instantly relaxed with each stroke. I found it particularly beneficial to massage her after her bath or shower at night. I always found that she slept especially well after a massage. I continued massaging her until she was about thirteen months old. This was our time: our chance to bond and connect in our own special way.

'I also showed my husband some strokes, which he still uses today on Ruby's feet. I have now come back to massage class with my new son Toby (aged ten weeks). Even though I remember most of the strokes, it is a great opportunity for us to have some special time together. He, like his sister, instantly relaxes, and he rewards me with a loving smile or chuckle when I touch him this way.

'At night, I once again massage my baby, but this time my other baby (now twenty-two months old) is sitting beside me mimicking my every stroke on her own baby doll!'

Brooke, mother of two

How to massage your baby

To massage your baby, lie him between your legs or on your lap, facing you, or kneel on the floor beside him – find a position that is comfortable for you both, and remember to connect with your baby before you begin to massage. It is important that you are relaxed, as your tension will be transferred to your baby. You can start massaging either your baby's head or feet first, but it is important to keep baby warm so if you undress him completely use a bunny rug to cover any body parts you aren't massaging.

> **82** *It is important that you are relaxed when you massage, as your tension will be transferred to your baby.*

As noted earlier, it is a good idea to attend infant massage classes or watch a DVD on the subject. Meanwhile, you can use the following strokes, in the order given, to give your baby a full body massage:

- Stroke the crown of baby's head in a gentle, circular motion. Then, with both hands, stroke with flat fingers from baby's brow to his temples. With your fingertips, massage in small circles around his jaw. If you are massaging a baby under six weeks old, avoid your baby's cheeks near his mouth or you'll trigger the rooting reflex and he will become frustrated as he tries to turn and grasp for food.

- Place both hands on baby's chest. With fingers flat, stroke outwards and down in a heart shape. Then stroke gently outwards over baby's shoulders. Next, cup your hands around his shoulders, using gentle circular motions with your thumbs. 'Milk' the arms from shoulder to fingertips and delicately massage your baby's hands and each of his fingers.

- With the palm of your hands, one hand following the other, stroke firmly around the tummy in clockwise circles (only after the cord has dropped off). This massage follows the colon and can be used to help relieve tummy ache (see below).

- Starting at the top of baby's thigh, 'milk' his legs, massage his ankles and then, supporting each ankle, use your thumb to massage along the sole of the foot. Give each toe a gentle rub.

- Place baby on his tummy, across your thighs. With one hand on his bottom (to make sure he doesn't roll off your lap), use your other hand to stroke from his shoulders towards his bottom. Finish off by lightly 'combing' his back with your fingertips, making slower and slower movements.

As you finish a massage, gradually lighten and slow your movements and then place your hands on your baby's back or stomach for a few moments: it may startle him if you stop massaging suddenly. As you rest your hands on your baby, continue the mood you have created by breathing slowly and feel the connection you have made. Keep his clothes ready so you can make dressing an extension of the massage, or roll him gently in a towel ready for a bath if this is your routine. And, of course, always enjoy a cuddle with your calm, relaxed baby after a massage!

> **83**   *As you finish a massage, gradually lighten and slow your movements and then place your hands on your baby's back or stomach for a few moments: it may startle your baby to stop massaging suddenly.*

Massage to tame tummy troubles

To move wind, encourage digestion and help ease tummy troubles resulting from gas or constipation, try the following massage sequence about twenty minutes after a breastfeed or forty minutes after a formula feed (if you don't feel confident, it would be worth watching my baby massage DVD – see Resources).

- Begin by resting your hands on your baby's tummy and connecting with him. With the palms of your hands moulded to baby's tummy, one above the other, horizontally, massage with one hand following the other 'paddling' downwards like a waterwheel (massaging upwards could make your baby vomit). Repeat six times.

- Gently bend your baby's knees up against his stomach and hold his legs for as long as he is comfortable, up to thirty seconds – this usually helps release trapped wind.

- Release baby's legs and stroke them from hip to ankle, coaxing your baby to 'relax, relax'.

- Next, with your palms, one hand following the other, stroke firmly around the tummy in continuous clockwise circles. Repeat these strokes six times.

- Bend baby's legs up again and hold them, then release and stroke.

- Repeat this sequence three times

If your baby has a regular 'crying time' or suffers from colic, try this routine about an hour before he is due to start his crying spell. To help your baby overcome colic, I recommend doing tummy massage twice a day for two weeks (after a morning feed when baby is content and again in the evening before his usual crying spell).

> **84** *To move wind, encourage digestion and help ease tummy troubles resulting from gas or constipation, try giving a tummy massage about twenty minutes after a breastfeed or forty minutes after a bottle-feed.*

Chapter nine
Coping (and not coping) with the crying

You need strength, energy and a (relatively) clear mind if you are to meet the unremitting demands of caring for a crying baby – for any baby, in fact. For your baby's sake, you also need all the practical help and support that is available. Yet your urge to protect your baby can isolate you from the very people who could provide your greatest support – even possibly your partner, because you are convinced he will not be able to pat your baby's bottom just so.

The irony is that often mothers of crying babies feel so inadequate that they dare not tell even their closest friends that they are having a difficult time, lest they are judged and fail to measure up. This conspiracy of silence that you must enter to convince others (and yourself) that you are 'coping' (whatever that means) can mean that you neglect the most important person in your baby's world – you!

'I think it was the fact that I had always been so independent that made it so much harder for me to surrender to these
feelings of vulnerability. I was a health professional – I felt I
should have known what to do. I couldn't see how normal it all
was to be tired, to cry more and to need help. I felt that everyone was always watching me – testing me – waiting for me to
slip up. Even amongst my girlfriends with babies, it felt like we
were all competing as to who was the "Perfect Mum with the
Perfect Baby".

'The more your baby seemed to cry, the more points you lost
and the more your confidence seemed to disappear. I had one
girlfriend who even refused to come to our playgroup because
she desperately didn't want the others to see her baby "lose
the plot" – interestingly, I don't ever remember her baby utter-
ing more than a squeak in all the times I saw her. Another
would breastfeed her baby constantly for the whole two hours
that we met, just so she didn't cry. Others would come, but
leave swiftly as soon as the baby even started to fuss only a
little. It became evident to me that these women felt that it was
not acceptable for others to see you or your baby get upset or
lose control. To be seen with a crying baby was to be seen as
an unsuccessful mother – and nobody wanted that.

'What is interesting is that at a recent dinner we all shared
we got a chance to talk out these feelings, two years on. Most

of the mothers felt safe enough now to admit how vulnerable and embarrassed they had all felt handling their "out of control" babies in front of each other. It was interesting how many of us had no idea how bad others in the group had been feeling during that time – we mourned the loss of both intimacy and support that we could have shared, if we had only felt safe enough to be vulnerable with each other.

'It was a huge relief to hear that others had felt the way I had. These were women who I greatly admired and respected as mothers, and so to hear them admit to similar feelings somehow made me feel like I had done an okay job after all. Those who have since had a second child commented that this need to "cover things up" and hide away had greatly diminished as time had passed and we had all become closer friends. With greater intimacy between us, they felt safer in letting us all see the "ugly" side of their lives and said that as a result they felt much calmer and confident in their mothering second time round.'

Melinda, mother of one

85 *The conspiracy of silence that you must enter to convince others (and yourself) that you are 'coping' (whatever that means) can mean that you neglect the most important person in your baby's world – you!*

Keep things in perspective

How did you imagine babies to be before one came to live at your house? More importantly, how did you see other parents before you became one – did you divide them into those who 'coped' and those who had allowed a baby to 'take over their lives'? Unfortunately, parenting is one job where effort doesn't necessarily equal outcome – which can be one of the hardest things to accept. As unfair as it may seem, some parents get the lucky dip when it comes to baby temperaments, health and wellbeing, while others face a much greater struggle.

The unpredictability of a crying baby's constant needs can make you feel out of control. It is logical, therefore, to expect that trying to solve your baby's problems, making plans and setting goals, will lift you out of the chaos. After all, this is the way we all work most efficiently in a child-free workplace. The problem is that being solution-focused doesn't equal efficiency where babies are concerned: you can't 'solve' a child. And even when we do find a solution to the current situation (that is, something that calms the crying for now), we tend to forget that infant development is a continuing process and so what works today is unlikely to be the answer tomorrow. Furthermore, what works for somebody else's baby may or may not work for yours. This, of course, means a lot of trial and error, which is neither efficient nor likely to provide an instant solution.

Even if we accept this current state of disorder, we promise ourselves that it is temporary – and the definition of temporary can often be very short indeed. As the reality sinks in and changes take longer than we anticipated (they said it would be easier at six weeks, three months, whatever), it is easy to become frustrated and to feel that life will never be the same, ever. The fact is that having a baby *is* a life-changing experience, whether or not you have been 'blessed' with a high-needs child.

Whatever your own feelings, your baby's needs have to take priority over yours. It is important to rationalise this and accept it, so that you don't let resentment ruin the bond between you and your baby.

One way to get the present phase into perspective is to take a piece of string and tie knots along it to represent each decade of your life. When you realise what a small portion of your life-span is actually going to be involved in this intensive parenting, you may find it easier to accept that although chaos reigns now it is really only for a short time in the overall scheme of things.

86 *Whatever your own feelings, your baby's needs have to take priority over yours. It is important to rationalise this and accept it, so that you don't let resentment ruin your bond.*

'Because we have moved from the communal set-up of tribal living into independent mothering, we are left alone to struggle with what at times can prove to be a very heavy load to carry. With no support or encouragement from others – such as older, wiser women – that this phase will pass, we see only the present situation of high dependency and no sleep as a continuum of the rest of our lives. If someone would just step forward and tell new mothers that it's okay to let go, it's okay to surrender – because it's not forever – then I believe more women would sit comfortably with the principles of nurturing their children through anything.'

Grace, mother of one

A maze of emotions

Although becoming a parent is a transforming event for both partners, mothers are generally affected more by emotional changes, simply because it is the mother who physically experiences giving birth and (because she has the breasts) she is the one with the least choice about how much she will participate in early parenting. Mothers are most likely to bear the effects of enforced fragmentation of time, sleep deprivation (both elements in torture) and contradictory advice. However, in spite of their comparative freedom, fathers can also find themselves in a state of emotional upheaval.

'For me, being a father is a personal growth journey, there is pain and joy and being able to acknowledge that, and being able to tolerate extremes of emotion, from amazingly joyous love to stress and anxiety and fear. When she was born, we became much more spontaneous, we planned less because planning became very difficult. Everything was purely about how the baby was, so we became much more in the here and now.'

Marcel, father of one

A sense of loss

Joining the parent '-hood' is exhilarating and, of course, has lots of wonderful moments, but at the same time there are also lots of losses – including your freedom, your sense of control, your financial independence and, for mothers, even the body you used to see in the mirror. Your relationships with family, friends and workmates and, most of all with your partner, are all changed dramatically. And this tends to be exacerbated if, on top of everything else, you have a crying baby.

The sum total of these losses can be a loss of identity, at least temporarily. This can be terrifying, as you are also coping with a whole new set of demands and expectations. Yet there is little acknowledgement of the see-sawing emotions that can affect both parents – except perhaps those experienced by the mother, but even this is usually seen as the influence of maternal hormones rather than emotional upheaval. Is it any wonder, then, that this trivialisation of legitimate grief also results in a loss of confidence for many women, especially if they are also mourning the non-appearance of the perfect (contented) baby they had come to anticipate in those media-influenced days BC (Before Child)?

'I was terrified of going out, and didn't really get over this until four months. Our first outing to the shops was at four weeks. It went really well at first, with Caitlin falling asleep in her pram and I felt unbelievably euphoric. I even felt confident enough to venture to the other end of the shopping centre from my car, to go to Myer. While we were in the babies' section,

Caitlin started crying and couldn't be settled. I thought I would have to go outside and walk around the perimeter of the shopping centre to get back to my car (no way was I going to walk through it). Then I spotted the mothers' room with (hurrah!) private cubicles. With extreme relief I locked us in one and fed my baby. Afterwards, though, she kept on crying for about 45 minutes, and I really did think that I was never going to leave the cubicle.

'Outings were still pretty infrequent for a while and our first grocery shop was at four months. I could handle the crying, but I couldn't handle the stares of others, or feeling that my skills as a mother (or more to the point, lack of) were on display for the world to see.'

Rochelle, mother of a nine-month-old

It is normal and valid to lament the loss of your former life, especially if parenthood has not met your expectations, no matter how unrealistic these were (you didn't plan to have a *crying* baby, did you?) You are not alone, you are not a 'bad parent' and you are not 'going crazy'. By giving yourself permission to consciously experience these feelings of loss and to acknowledge them, you will also be able to work through them and adapt more easily to your changed circumstances. If you are missing your old social life, for instance, you can try to replace this in a new way by social-ising with other new parents: with babies in tow, take turns having dinner together at each others' homes (each take a dish to share). Or, if you feel socially restricted by your crying baby, why not take her along to a 'cry baby' session at your local cinema (these are special showings of current movies especially for parents accompanied by babies). And if – having put baby before briefcase (or before overseas trips/long working hours/a larger pay packet) – you are missing the sense of achievement you used to get from a fast-paced career, try to work out how you can address this in your new role. You may need to do some redefining and reassessing of your 'old' attitudes and values, but denying your feelings will only prolong your adjustment and will certainly prevent you from reaching out for support.

87   *If you feel socially restricted by your crying baby, why not take her along to a 'cry baby' session at your local cinema.*

'When I look back on my parenting experiences with Joshua, my first child, twelve years ago, the main thing I remember was the incessant crying and the difficulty I had dealing with it at the time. I was young, ill-prepared for the realities of parenthood and quite unsupported. I felt alone and angry. How

can a young baby cry and cry and cry? I almost believed that I was being punished and that I was not a good parent. I was supposed to enjoy motherhood. I held an idealised image of motherhood – I should be in control, able to manage everything and the baby would be happy. The reality was very different. I ended up submerging into two years of depression. I loved Joshua more than anything in the world, but this was an exceptionally difficult chapter in my life.

'Ten years after Joshua's birth I found myself pregnant again with a much-wanted baby. Pregnancy was fabulous – this time I had a wonderful support network. I was excited about the prospect of labour and birth and meeting my new child. I was scared, though, scared of how I was going to cope with motherhood a second time. Scared that this baby would be like Joshua and cry excessively.

'When Jarred entered this world, he entered with a howl. Jarred was very unsettled for the first 24 hours of his life (it took him this long to actually get to sleep). I thought: Oh my goodness, what have I done? Some of the old feelings started to arise, then I thought, Well, I can't alter Jarred's behaviour; I can only alter my own reaction to his behaviour. I moved into a phase of acceptance. Even though Jarred was a very unsettled baby, my attitude was so totally different. I felt relaxed and accepting of the situation and for the most part thoroughly

*enjoyed being a mother for the second time. It certainly chal-
lenged me, but we found our way through it and by three
months of age Jarred was a relatively calm baby and I was a
happy mother. Jarred wasn't a great sleeper (he still isn't at
eighteen months of age), but I became creative about dealing
with the situation. I did what I needed to. At times I rocked him
to sleep in a pram or carried him in a pouch. I breastfed him
to sleep frequently. I played relaxing music. I set little routines.
I tried suggestions from friends, health professionals or books.
I basically used trial and error.*

*'I am now hoping that Jarred and Joshua will have a new
brother and sister in the near future. This time I will look forward to the prospect of being a mother of a new baby.'*

Jane, mother of two

Anger

Research shows that a baby's crying actually raises the
blood pressure of people listening to it, so it is hardly sur-
prising that hours of crying can be a trigger for parental
anger. Frustration that your baby is disrupting your life or
rejecting your efforts to provide care can quite easily slip
over the line into anger or rage. The intensity of your emotions can be frightening, but this doesn't make you a bad
parent. It does, though, mean you need help.

88 *Frustration that your baby is disrupting your life or rejecting your efforts to provide care can quite easily slip over the line into anger or rage. This doesn't make you a bad parent. It does, though, mean you need help.*

Get a grip on yourself before you get a grip on your baby

If your baby's crying is getting to you, and you feel so stressed or angry that you fear you might cause her harm, walk away. Lie your baby in her cot and then leave the room, closing the door behind you. Turn on the radio, wear earplugs, take a shower, go outside or lie down in another room where you can't hear her, and take some deep slow breaths. Most importantly, call someone who cares – your partner, your mother, a friend or a help line.

No matter how frustrated you feel about her crying, never, ever shake your baby. This could cause permanent, irreparable brain damage, or even death.

'Sienna had been crying for three days. I was at the end of my tether, so I put her in her cot and made myself a cup of coffee. I was standing in the garden drinking it when I heard my six-year-old's voice behind me saying, "You are a bad mother to

let her cry." I picked the cup up and hurled it at the back fence. Then I took a few deep breaths and picked my baby up and drove her to the children's hospital. I probably should never have driven a car in such a distraught state, but, of course, by the time we got to the hospital the car ride had calmed her down and she had stopped crying. They couldn't find anything wrong with her.'

Andrea, mother of two

89 *No matter how frustrated you feel about his crying, never, ever, shake your baby. This could cause permanent, irreparable brain damage, or even death.*

Guilt

Most men seem better able to rationalise and justify their actions than their partners. The art of self-flagellation is as synonymous with motherhood as stretchmarks – and equally difficult to eradicate: most of us find it difficult not to allow our guilty feelings to run rampant whenever we fail to live up to our images of the perfect parent (and whenever our child fails to measure up to the image of the 'good' baby who, of course, is a reflection of our own competence).

Faced with the stresses of parenthood, especially a crying baby and a lack of sleep, it is easy to make choices that are not those we might have made if we had more resources (information, support, time, money, energy) available to us at the time. However, this is not something to feel guilty about: guilt is only really legitimate if you let another person down, if you haven't honestly done all that you could have. Sometimes, we try to blame our feelings of guilt on others – 'They made me feel guilty' – but whatever external factors trigger your feelings of guilt, these are *your* feelings. You need to decide whether this guilt is justifiable or not – even whether it is, in fact, guilt or some other emotion – and how you will act on the feeling.

The positive thing about guilt is that you can act on it: if you feel guilty about the choices you are making, you can use these feelings to motivate you to make better choices. However, the downside to beating up on yourself is that you can miss out on precious present moments by concentrating your energy on what you *should* have done.

If you *are* feeling guilt, it can be helpful to ask yourself: Where is this feeling coming from? Is this the best I can do for now, or am I really letting my child down? What can I change?

Depression

See-sawing emotions, guilt, frustration and feelings of inadequacy all come within the normal range of emotions for most mothers in the early weeks (or months), especially if you are struggling with a crying baby and sleepless nights. But if you ever feel so inadequate that you consistently think your baby deserves another mother, or that your family would be better off without you, these are serious warning signs that you could be suffering from postnatal depression. This is a medical illness, not evidence that you can't cope.

There is no single factor that has been identified as a cause of postnatal depression. Rather, it is thought to be the product of several interrelated biochemical, psychological and social factors. And if you are wondering where the normal maze of maternal emotions ends and the black tunnel of depression begins, the difficult thing is that most women don't simply wake up one morning with postnatal depression – it can even develop slowly over several months. Symptoms may include sleep and appetite disturbance, chronic exhaustion or hyperactivity, loss of memory or concentration, and anxiety or panic. The debilitating exhaustion characteristic of depressive illness will affect your ability to enjoy your baby and may also affect your ability to respond appropriately. This, in turn, may result in a vicious circle of more baby (and mother) crying, which will increase your own feelings of inadequacy.

Postnatal depression affects the entire family unit, and some men who have cared for partners with postnatal depression have themselves become so run-down that they too became prone to depression. So, please consider that extreme tiredness or irritability may not simply be a result of sleepless nights and a difficult baby, but symptoms of a treatable illness. Discuss your thoughts and feelings (no matter how bizarre) with your doctor and/or child health nurse, so they can offer appropriate diagnosis and treatment. And if you have difficulty getting help or a sympathetic hearing, take a friend or your partner to the doctor to support you, or call one of the relevant organisations listed at the back of this book (see 'Postnal Depression' in the Resources section).

90 *If you ever feel so inadequate that you consistently think your baby deserves another mother, or that your family would be better off without you, these are serious warning signs that you could be suffering from postnatal depression. This is a medical illness, not evidence that you can't cope.*

'I was absolutely physically exhausted with twins, a toddler and a child just starting school. The babies were nineteen months old when I realised I had postnatal depression. Where normally I would bounce out of bed, have a shower and put my make-up on, as the depression set in I couldn't face getting out of bed. When I heard them cry in the morning I would have a panic attack, thinking, "Oh, no, my day has begun." I was so bone-tired, I felt I couldn't face another day. My personal grooming had gone out the window – forget make-up! Another early symptom was that I lost my sense of taste. Often, I would sit in the twins' room, just crying. About three weeks into this, I realised I needed help. Luckily I had good support networks of family and friends. The important thing to know is that it does get better.'

Eve, mother of four, including twins

'I could see Beth unravelling. She was more and more "down". She was screaming at me. One day she lost it and screamed and screamed. This was so unlike her. I felt she was out of control but I couldn't make anything better, no matter what I did. I found it hard with two children to care for.

'When I took Beth to hospital, I felt responsible for her illness. She had become ill so gradually that even when I had the hospital interview, I didn't realise how seriously ill she was.

I felt like everything was cast adrift. While she was in hospital I attended a fathers' group there once a week. I never looked too far ahead. I did think she would get better – it was so new to me and I didn't know anyone who had had postnatal depression, so I didn't know it could go on for ages. She had always been such a capable person that I just assumed she would be again – and thankfully, she is. But I do feel our oldest child suffered from the separation. I had just started a new job, so he stayed with my mother and he would scream and scream when I visited him. Even now, three years later, we can't leave him with my mum.'

Paul, father of two

When you're losing those loving feelings

Under the stress of a high-needs baby, the definition of 'shared parenting' can become very blurred. One or other parent may feel as though they are being expected to do more than is humanly possible, and feel resentful. It is easy, too, for fathers to justify working longer hours ('We need the money, honey'); but, Dad, be honest with yourself – is it really that work offers a 'legitimate' escape from the chaos at home, or perhaps provides a place where you can again feel in control and confident about your role?

It is also common for fathers to feel resentful of the shift in their partner's attention, away from them to the crying baby. The best way to solve this is for fathers to offer support and practical help, so that there is some time (and loving feelings) left to share once baby's needs have been attended to.

Mothers too can be 'at fault' here – there is nothing like a helpless, crying baby to bring out the 'mother lioness' in any one of us. It is normal, too, for mothers to be more upset by crying because of their natural physiological response. This ferocious protectiveness can mean that mothers unintentionally push away fathers by relegating them to the status of apprentice rather than partner. Fathers may not handle the baby the same way you do, and sometimes they are a little less 'in tune' with baby's cues since they are not usually there all the time, but does it really make a difference to the crying? Or are you being unnecessarily critical and risking the withdrawal of your best ally?

91 *Your partner may not handle the baby the same way you do, but does it really make a difference to the crying? Or are you being unnecessarily critical and risking the withdrawal of your best ally?*

'Georgia's crying was very trying for both my partner and myself, and we suffered severely from lack of sleep for a couple of weeks. There was name-calling and once he even deliberately stomped on my foot! The evenings were always fussy and sometimes I just held Georgia while she cried, as nothing would stop her. Sam would often give me evil looks and mutter under his breath about why I wasn't doing anything. I didn't do anything because there was simply nothing left to do!'

Elise, mother of one

'The biggest mistake I think that my hub and I made was blaming each other for our baby not being able to sleep and not taking up offers from others for time out.'

Cindy, mother of a four-month-old

'I have an Early Childhood teaching background and have a twenty-month-old and a two-month-old. Everyone, including my partner, assumes I know what to do and how to cope, no matter what. I spend many hours alone with the children and constantly recall my knowledge of child development to cope. Patience, flexibility, time management and organisation are strengths, but nothing – and I mean nothing – beats the support of a loving husband who reaches out to give a hug or a smile or even a great home-cooked meal to help deal with the cry of a baby and a toddler. We all want to feel like the old person we were prior to children.'

Anna, mother of two

'From my viewpoint as a dad I still had some far-off Neanderthal urge to say, "Will you shut that kid up!" Not only is this a negative and sexist view, but it makes the baby cry even more because they pick up on the bad vibes going on. I soon found that babies cry for a reason, and for that reason need to be comforted with touch, voice and love. They need to know that you are there with your devotion to make whatever is upsetting them go away. I kept in my head at the time a picture of what she would look like asleep, and one of a peaceful surrounding, i.e. beach, paddock, etc. If this didn't work it still kept me calm. I rocked and hummed, I cuddled, I wrapped her up tightly, and on rare occasions I have sat on the floor rocking the cot for hours at a time. I was always trying to achieve a goal, peace for my child. If it all got too hard, I would walk away and ask Kristy to take over, or Mum or Dad, whoever was there. Sometimes your baby might need someone else, not you this time. I soon learnt not to take this personally. Don't let it get that bad that you could hurt or injure your child. If it does get to that stage, put her down and walk away for a while and get someone to help you.'

Tom, father of one

It is vital during this difficult time to communicate honestly with your partner and work out how to support each other: although tension is almost inevitable when you are exhausted and stressed, and blaming each other for your baby's distress is common among parents of a crying baby, you can hardly expect a calm baby in the midst of a stormy relationship.

To avoid arguments, try to express your fears and frustration without blaming or accusing, and listen carefully to what your partner is trying to say. Don't forget to show appreciation for helpful gestures, and do try to create special moments of connection with each other: even if you are too stuffed for a romp in the sack, give each other hugs, hold hands as you pound the footpaths to soothe the sobs, or slump together on the couch.

If you feel dissatisfied, distrustful or can't talk any more, outside help is probably called for. It may just take a couple of sessions with a counsellor to set you on the right track – it's not a slur on your ability to cope and it may save your relationship.

92 *Although tension is almost inevitable when you are exhausted and stressed, and blaming each other for your baby's distress is common among parents of a crying baby, you can hardly expect a calm baby in the midst of a stormy relationship.*

Sibling harmony

Imagine: your partner has just brought home a new lover and announced that you are all going to live together – it will be fun, you will be best friends! After hearing that you and the new lover will be loved equally by your partner, you are asked to share your things (all of them) with the new lover. It also turns out that you won't be getting as much attention as you used to, because the new lover is a bit upset about something and anyway you are such a clever person that you can do lots of things by yourself now. Oh, and by the way, you must be gentle with the new lover! Is it any wonder your older child feels displaced?

If a lot of your time is spent consoling a crying baby, as well as helping an older child adjust to a new sibling, you can feel as though you are splitting apart – rather like a piece of meat being fought over between a pair of voracious puppies. This is one time where any help at all should be gratefully accepted – if you have a free hand (or a silent spell) to pick up the phone! Meanwhile, here are a few suggestions that may help smooth this tricky time:

- Give your older child a small album of photos taken when he was a baby, and chat about them with him. This can be a great time to mention, 'When you used to

cry, we gave you lots of cuddles [you used to like walk-
ing/mummy singing/riding in the car, or whatever].'

- Let your older children help while you feed, change,
wash, hold or massage the baby – it might be more 'helpful' to give your older child a doll so that he can feed and
dress 'his' baby while you attend to the real one.

- Set up a corner for feeding and crying times, with special things to occupy your toddler: snacks and drinks
(make up a lunchbox in quiet times and keep it in the
fridge for when baby feeds or crying times intrude on
toddler meal-times – life is easier if your older child's
blood sugar levels are stable), storybooks, playing
cards, paper dolls, scrapbook and crayons, a CD player
with story CDs or favourite action songs, or pop a few
interesting little things like cards or Matchbox toys
(and perhaps a small snack pack or juice box) into
brown-paper lunch bags and bring out a surprise bag
as a diversion for desperate moments.

- Make an effort to notice and encourage your older
child's positive behaviour.

- When the baby is contented, or perhaps as she (finally)
dozes off to sleep, tell her (within earshot of the older
sibling) that you and your older child are going to do
something special together – paint a picture, play with

playdough, have a swing – but that babies are *much* too little for such a fun activity.

- Don't give the baby treasured items – favourite blankets, toys – that belong to the older child, without asking first.

- Introduce big changes (such as moving from a cot to a bed, or starting preschool) either well before the baby arrives or several months later. An unsettled new baby and the ensuing family upheaval is enough adjustment at one time – even for parents!

- Regression and resentment are normal reactions to the shift in your attention from your older child to the 'disruptive' newcomer. If your older child voices negative feelings about the baby, show understanding by saying something like, 'It sounds like you're mad at the baby, maybe because she has been crying a lot and needing so much of my time.' Let the child talk honestly about his feelings, but make it clear that it is not acceptable to hurt the baby.

'Even though I was terribly close to our first child, Beau, and was very aware of not having him feel left out as a result of my spending too much time with our new baby, I still had been consumed somewhat by Jacob. With breastfeeding, work

commitments and home duties – it seemed when I did have any spare time I was absolutely exhausted. Too exhausted to spend the time with Beau that I used to. It seemed having a new baby around had turned my "other baby" into this back-chatting, defiant, mess-making "big boy" who left the toilet seat up, wouldn't clean his room and created more washing than all the kids who lived in the old woman's shoe put together!

'But having to be away from Beau for a recent business trip overseas brought with it much grief and pulled me back into reality. All of a sudden something "clicked" and our lives seemed to instantly revert to the way things used to be. Beau seemed (or was it he felt that I subconsciously "allowed" him) to once again become the "little" cute, sensitive, helpful and very beautiful soul he had always been. I remembered how great it felt to sit him on my knee and hold him close, how he had cried with me when we found out I was pregnant, the look on his face at the birth of his new brother … It all began to make sense, he had had his mother to himself for six long years, and as much as he loved this new baby, it seemed to take me away from him. I can look back and realise how the birth must have impacted our first child, in that he must have felt he was "losing" his mum, so to speak, for that short time. Now, I have two beautiful little souls who fill my life – some-times with tears, but they are tears of joy!'

Catherine, mother of two

Nurture yourself

Parents deserve to be nurtured too. This is easy to forget as you wander about with your eyes hanging out from exhaustion as you meet your baby's constant needs. And even if you are craving care and comfort, it can be difficult to feel at ease about taking time off to take care of yourself (or even to rest and eat properly) as you look around and notice all the things you *should* be doing. Your own health and sense of wellbeing have an enormous ripple effect on the entire family, though, so it is important to take steps to maintain your energy and your temper.

> **93** *Your own health and sense of wellbeing have an enormous ripple effect on the entire family, so it is important to take steps to maintain your energy and your temper.*

Naps aren't just for babies

If you are suffering from interrupted sleep (or barely any sleep at all), take 'catch-up' naps – even a fifteen-minute power nap will refresh you when you are flagging. And learn how to breastfeed lying down: dozing as you feed is good for your milk supply as well as your energy levels. In the early weeks, especially, rest when your baby does: make up a sign 'Mother and Baby Resting' and hang it on the door with a notepad so visitors can leave a message.

> **94** In the early weeks, especially, rest when your baby does: make up a sign 'Mother and Baby Resting' and hang it on the door with a notepad so visitors can leave a message.

Slow down!

Learning to pace yourself will help you conserve energy too. Although it may be tempting to race around on 'good' days (or as your baby sleeps), this is likely to deplete your reserves even further. So don't knock yourself out trying to clean the whole house from top to bottom while she is asleep, only to find you are exhausted by the time she wakes up. Divide your workload: plan one large job each day, such as cleaning the fridge or the bathroom, or tidying one shelf.

Pacing yourself also means prioritising invitations to potentially tiring events and planning to have a nap in the afternoon before an evening outing, or possibly arranging a babysitter for a few hours the next day so you can have a catch-up nap.

Eat to boost your energy

- **Never skip breakfast:** Give yourself a head start in the energy stakes, and maintain your energy levels until the afternoon, by eating a nutritious breakfast.

- **Eat plenty of magnesium-rich foods:** Magnesium has been called nature's relaxant, so the flow-on effect, if you are breastfeeding, may be a calmer baby. Magnesium-rich foods include green foods such as leafy vegetables, seaweed and algae products; nuts and seeds (take care with peanuts if breastfeeding, as they are a common allergen); whole-grain cereals; and soy and dairy products.

- **Avoid 'empty' calories:** Sweets and junk food will not sustain your energy and may cause mood changes as your blood sugar levels fluctuate. Opt for healthy snacks such as fresh fruit or vegetables, and small easy meals containing protein such as eggs, cheese and crackers, or tuna sandwiches.

- **Feed on fish or take fish-oil capsules:** Deep-sea fish such as salmon, tuna and mackerel are rich in DHA, an omega-3 fatty acid important in maintaining the nervous system. Studies show that a mother's DHA levels become depleted as her body provides for the developing infant during pregnancy and breastfeeding, and low levels of **DHA** can lead to reduced concentrations of serotonin, which has been linked to postnatal depression.

- ✎ **Take a good multivitamin:** There are some specially formulated for new mothers.

- ✎ **Drink plenty of water:** Fatigue is one of the first and most common signs of dehydration. Heed your body signals, drink whenever you breastfeed your baby, and at mealtimes, and carry a water bottle with you when you go out (if you have the energy!)

95 *Eat plenty of magnesium-rich foods. Magnesium has been called nature's relaxant, so the flow-on effect, if you are breastfeeding, may be a calmer baby.*

'I would call my partner during the afternoon to ask him what time he would be home. I felt so exhausted and light headed, I couldn't bear the thought of him arriving home a minute late. Invariably he would hear the desperation in my voice and he would ask, "When did you last eat?"

'Sometimes I hadn't eaten for several hours, simply because I was flat-out attending to the little ones, and obviously my blood sugar was low, but because of this, I could barely think straight enough to realise why I felt so depleted (low blood

sugar actually does make you feel confused). He would tell me
to go and eat, then call him back in half an hour. I was usually
coping again by then. I just hadn't realised I needed to eat
so much more frequently because I was breastfeeding a baby
and a toddler.'

Ellie, mother of two

Give yourself a break

However impossible it might seem when you have a high-
needs baby, it's essential to give yourself a regular break –
to relax (at least occasionally) and to laugh. (If there isn't
a funny side to your own life at the moment, hire a good
comedy DVD: you can stop and start it between the
wails.)

You may feel that the organisation required even to
take a few hours off is an added stress, depending on your
support networks. But the point is that you need nurturing *every* day, and this is possible even if you can't manage
blocks of 'time out'. Try to be kind to yourself and do at
least one thing each day that makes you feel good: buy
yourself a magazine: you can read it as you feed your baby
if this is the only time he is quiet – he can't cry *and* eat.
Buy yourself a bunch of flowers (don't dwell on the sad
state of affairs you're in, buying your own), just pick your

favourites and enjoy them. (Partners, take note!) Paint your toenails – unlike fingernails, if the baby wakes they won't be smudged. (Hint: use express-drying nail polish.) Or buy yourself some luxurious bubble bath or massage oil and ask your partner to help you use it.

If free time really is at a premium, or you are home alone with baby, learn to give yourself five-minute breaks – make up a list of things you can do in five minutes, or make a copy of the suggestions below and post it on the fridge to remind yourself:

- Read an article
- Do some exercise
- Call a friend
- Meditate
- Practise deep-breathing and stretching
- Put on a CD
- Have a (healthy) snack
- Clean out your handbag
- Write a postcard
- Send an email

One way to get yourself little chunks of time is to share child care with another mum. If you feel uneasy about leaving your baby, invite the other mother to your place so she can watch your baby while you have a rest; this way, you will be close by if the other mother gets overwhelmed by caring for two little ones. Consider putting up a notice at the baby health clinic to find a new friend who also understands the challenges of a crying baby (why not start a crying babies group?) But don't feel you can't approach an existing friend who has an easy baby: she may feel humbled by helping you and if she is a *real* friend she will accept and love your baby, wails and all!

> 'I used to share one day a week with a friend. We would take turns going to each other's homes and cooking a few meals to stock the freezer. One of us was always free to hold a baby or watch a toddler, and our partners would come to that home for dinner. As our babies grew, we spent less time together because we worked part-time, but we used the same arrangement to spend a day taking the children to a local orchard, or berry picking, and then we would make jam together.'
>
> **Lisa, mother of three**

Simplify, simplify . . .

Although your baby's needs do have to come before the state of the floor or how many dishes are left to eat off, if you feel overwhelmed by the chaos of a disorganised (messy) house, this stress won't help you or your crying baby. The golden rule is, 'Simplify, simplify, simplify.' Here are a few suggestions:

- **Hire yourself some help:** Yes, it does cost money, but even one thorough house-clean, or one basket of ironing outsourced can relieve the pressure.
- **Don't shop till you drop:** Make fewer shopping trips, or do away with shopping excursions altogether by having groceries and fruit and vegetables home-delivered – if you have access to the Internet, you can order practically anything on-line, from groceries to gifts.
- **Combine baby care with housework:** Wear baby in a sling as you do chores. She'll enjoy the ride and the view, and be soothed by the movement, and you'll get extra jobs done. And then you'll feel freer to take a catnap when she sleeps.

96 *Combine baby care with housework by wearing baby in a sling as you do chores. She'll enjoy the ride and the view, and be soothed by the movement, and you'll get extra jobs done.*

Reach out

In those carefree days before baby arrived, you were probably proud of your independence. This new life (the inconsolable little one in your arms) depends on you totally and that awesome responsibility can see you desperate for back-up, whether it is reassurance that you are doing everything you possibly can to alleviate your baby's distress, or real hands-on practical help. For your baby's sake, it is important to reach out and buffer yourself with a cushion of support to keep you from spiralling into isolation and despair.

Nowadays, the 'wise women' (including your own mother) who would have traditionally supported new mothers are likely to be off doing their own thing – meeting corporate deadlines, studying, or travelling far away. So, rather than relying on these traditional networks, we each need to establish our own support systems. Although it is best to begin doing this before your baby arrives, it is never too late, and as your child grows you will find your buffer zone evolves to meet your changing needs.

Your support network could include a good friend who will give you and your baby hugs when you need them, a playgroup, a voluntary support group (most offer free telephone counselling), or professionals such as the family GP – and a whole range of people in between. The Internet can also be a handy source of information and encouragement: although it isn't the same as face-to-face (or voice-to-voice) contact, and the advice you receive can be questionable at times, it can be comforting to communicate with other suffering parents who can at least offer support or commiseration at three in the morning. And if you really feel like venting your frustration, you can always remain anonymous.

If you can juggle a pen and a fractious baby, it is a good idea to make a checklist of the sorts of support that would be most helpful to you (see the Resources section for suggestions). Then make up a list of names (with contact details) to post on the wall near your phone, where it will be handy in an emergency. And if you are desperate and you feel as though you have been dismissed by somebody you've called, don't give up – call the next person on your list.

'I wasted hours isolated at home as I tried to get my baby into a routine. Eventually, I worked out that if the baby wouldn't sleep anyway, you may as well be out with friends rather than being miserably locked up in your house with an unsettled baby (and

usually the little darling would sleep soundly in his capsule while I told people how I'd been up all night).'

Isabelle, mother of one

'Sam still has bad days, and after attending to all possible reasons for crying, I tend to pack him up in the car and visit "baby-experienced" family or friends. This gets both of us out of the house and into a different environment. Again, sometimes this works and sometimes it is a dead loss. Also, this option only is good for daylight hours. As much as my mum loves Sam, a 1 a.m. visit is not a good idea.'

Julie, mother of a six-week-old

Ask for help – and accept it

Although it can be relatively easy to vent your pent up feelings to an anonymous person on the phone, most of us find it difficult to actually ask even those closest to us for practical help. The sad thing about carrying the load by ourselves is that most people feel privileged to share in the magic of a baby, so throw off those inhibitions and speak up – be open to receiving help, and conserve your energy to care for your child.

It is worth bearing in mind that sometimes the price of help may be an earful of well-meant but irrelevant advice. So weigh up the value of advice versus help, practise your assertiveness techniques (see 'A little advice goes a long way' on page 28) or be creative about finding help – it can be found in all sorts of unexpected ways. When I had our second child, we had a twelve-year-old neighbour who adored our toddler, so she used to come and play with the two-year-old while I walked and fed and changed the baby, who seemed to need a marathon evening feed (all evening). When our youngest child was born, he had an eleven-year-old sister who was a perfect little 'mummy'. Girls around this age seem to love babies and can quite safely be allowed to sit in a rocking chair cuddling your infant, or on the floor playing with an older baby, if there is a watchful eye close by. If you know a young girl who likes babies, invite her over to play with your baby as you cook dinner, whip round with the vacuum cleaner, or make a few phone calls. Or offer her money to do some light chores like bringing in and folding washing or helping you tidy up. Kids generally can't get paid work until they are at least fifteen, but they are capable of giving useful help long before then – just don't abuse their good will or burden them with sole responsibility for a baby or toddler: they don't deserve the guilt that comes with an 'If only' (my child hadn't choked, drowned or run onto the road).

> **97** *Most people feel privileged to share in the magic of a baby, so throw off those inhibitions and speak up – be open to receiving help, and conserve your energy to care for your child.*

'My baby had been crying for hours – at least that is what it seemed like. I was crying as loud as he was. My partner was away, and my mother was away, so I called my godmother. It was such a difficult thing to ask for help, but she came over straight away. She sat with my baby in the rocking chair with him across her lap and just patted his back and rocked. And he stopped crying. He must have sensed she was completely calm, where I was absolutely distraught.'

Vicki, mother of one

When you need a (detached) expert

Seeking some casual help or support to survive the crying times is one thing. But if you are becoming distraught and overwhelmed by your baby's crying, it may be wise to call in an expert who can offer some baby-handling know-how or reassurance. You can draw on the range of support groups in the Resources section at the back of this book, or you can seek professional help (which, of course, usually involves financial costs). Such professionals may include:

Maternal and child health nurses

You don't have to attend your local clinic if you prefer a nurse in another area – some will have extra qualifications. Baby health nurses are well informed about infant development. A good nurse will be able to help with feeding, crying and sleep issues as well as being able to support you with your own health and adjustment to motherhood. Many nurses organise groups for new mothers where you will meet women with babies the same age as yours and support each other as you deal with the same problem. Your nurse is part of a large network of other resources so she can refer you elsewhere if you have concerns about any aspect of your baby's development that she cannot address. It will also help to keep an after-hours number handy. Even though the after-hours nurse won't be the person who is familiar with your baby she will have lots of experience and expertise about babies, and it is reassuring to know you can contact a professional in the middle of the night.

A midwife

If you had a midwife in private practice for your baby's birth, you could call her and ask for help or advice. Or you can call the hospital where your baby was born – hospitals are staffed around the clock, and even if the person you speak to doesn't remember (or never met) you, they will be able to offer some tips to help you calm the crying if you are in the middle of a crisis.

> **98** *If you are becoming distraught and overwhelmed by your baby's crying, it may be wise to call in an expert who can offer some baby-handling know-how or reassurance.*

A lactation consultant

Lactation consultants offer specialist breastfeeding support and assistance. Many are employed in hospital maternity wards or mother–baby units, or in specialised clinics where mothers and babies with breastfeeding problems can spend a few hours or a day. Many maternal and child health nurses and independent midwives are also certified lactation consultants. Some lactation consultants work in private practice and will make home visits to help with feeding and settling issues – this is a boon if you are having difficulty finding the letterbox, let alone the car keys, with a crying baby in tow.

Be sure to check that the person you consult has IBCLC (International Board of Certified Lactation Consultants) qualifications and is a member of a recognised professional body, such as the Australian Lactation Consultants Association and the International Lactation Consultants Association.

> **99** *Some lactation consultants work in private practice and will make home visits to help with feeding and settling issues – this is a boon if you are having difficulty finding the letterbox, let alone the car keys, with a crying baby in tow.*

Doulas

The role of a doula is to help *you*, not to solve your baby's feeding or crying problems. The word doula is derived from a Greek word meaning mother's servant. This pretty much explains the role of a doula, who may offer services ranging from birth support to practical postnatal help. When you employ a doula, you can define what help is most suited to you – from help with housework or shopping to minding the baby while you catch up on some sleep, either during the day or even overnight. Although there are no national standards for doula training, there are several training providers so you will need to do your homework and ask what is offered and what qualifications your prospective doula has. Some doulas will have extra qualifications or experience and will offer services accordingly, such as breastfeeding counselling or massage.

Mother–baby units

These are often attached to maternity units in private hospitals. Some offer day stays to observe you feed and handle your baby. Trained staff can address any feeding problems and help you finetune skills such as reading your baby's cues and offer a few pointers. Others will take you and your baby for several days. This can be a good option that allows you to focus on your baby and feel supported, without the added responsibility of running your household. A word of caution, though: some of these centres use 'baby training' programmes with little or no consideration for the individual needs of the baby – in other words, they offer variations of the 'cry it out' approach. You will probably be at peak vulnerability by the time you approach such a facility and may find it difficult to resist once you are in its unfamiliar and possibly intimidating environment. It may help to assess exactly what your objectives are (and those of the centre) before you discover you have booked into a 'baby boot camp'.

> *'My daughter is nearly nine months and for the past two months or so has been having sleep problems at night. She was waking regularly and taking quite a bit to resettle. A friend recommended that I try a sleep school. Well, I did and it has been an absolute disaster. My daughter is now so distraught that she screams when we try to put her to sleep. She won't sleep during the day (literally) and at night will go into the cot after a bottle (very drowsy) but when she wakes in the night again she screams for hours. She can be awake for three to four hours at a time and is soooooo upset. Yesterday she had only six and a half hours sleep for the WHOLE day. I left the sleep school on Tuesday and when I rang them, distraught, they said that I have to be patient and it should work out, but I hate seeing my daughter this way. She screamed for the whole week she was at sleep school, too.'*

Marlee, mother of one

Often, the success of any regimen to settle babies owes more to the fact that the downward spiral of despair is interrupted, and mothers feel supported, than to any magic answers. The fact that parents feel understood and supported can be enough to remove tension and instil confidence. In fact, once you have ruled out health or feeding problems, a weekend at a **B&B** – in a remote country location, out of earshot of anyone who may offer unhelpful advice! – could be almost as helpful for parents and babies.

Chapter ten
Blessings

'I had left my own baby Jacob for the first time in sixteen months to go on a business trip to Korea. I was a little emotional and so looking forward to seeing my boys it consumed my every thought...

'When I boarded the plane for the trip home, I heard a young baby crying inconsolably. Then I realised I was sitting next to this baby. During the next few minutes the parents and I exchanged a few words – I mentioned my having left Jacob at home and the business I am in – hoping this would offer them some relief in case they were worried about annoying fellow passengers. It turned out they had been worried, dreading the trip – wondering about whom they would be sitting alongside. This couple from Australia had just travelled to Korea, to collect a little baby they'd adopted who had been given up at two weeks old by his fifteen-year-old mum. The baby – Liam, they called him – had only even been with a foster mum.

'Liam's new parents were only given half an hour to spend with him before the trip home. Wow – my heart was breaking.

This little baby cried so hard, tears simply poured down his face. It was extremely difficult for me not to get upset. I continued to look out the window (thank goodness I had a window seat) when I felt my own tears well up. When more than half an hour had passed, the plane still hadn't taken off and the baby was still crying his little eyes out, I finally plucked up enough courage to ask if I could hold their baby: knowing they had only spent a short, precious time with Liam, I was very aware of not coming across too confident or imposing on these very special moments for them. I commented it must be so beautiful to finally be able to take him home ... They agreed, passing him over almost with a sense of relief. I don't think I've ever seen a baby cry so much – mine never did. I couldn't imagine how the parents must be feeling, but I knew how I was feeling.

'Anyway, knowing I was just "another strange face" to this baby didn't deter me. I held this baby close to my heart with both arms and gently patted his bottom, spoke in whispers and rocked him. I'm not terribly religious, but I prayed silently for some peace for this little boy who had already undergone such trauma in his short life. I prayed for his new parents, for support and confidence in their new role as parents. Within a few minutes baby Liam was sleeping peacefully in my arms. The joy I felt was overwhelming.

'The aircraft personnel moved the parents and baby, and I don't know why but they also moved me, to new seats which they thought would be more comfortable. I held Liam all the while and placed him in the bassinette where he slept the entire ten hours home, woke twice for a feed and play and then went peacefully back to sleep. The parents were so very grateful and it was a fulfilling experience for me. So, always remember a little love from a stranger can go a long way…'

Catherine, mother of two

Perhaps the stares your baby's crying elicits from perfect strangers aren't always glares of disapproval or judgement: it is natural to feel sensitive when your best efforts to protect your child seem less than perfect, but could it be possible that many of the stares and whispers that surround you and your crying baby are really voices of concern or even deeply felt empathy? After all, empathy (along with humility) can be one of the greatest lessons learned by parents who have a crying baby.

You have two choices when your baby cries: to respond, or to ignore the cries. By responding, you are not only teaching your baby to love, you too are learning about the greatest love of all – unconditional love: you are accepting the child you have in your arms just the way he is. There are many points along the continuum of parenthood when it is easy to wish our child was just a little (or a lot) more 'this' or 'that' (easier in some way, depending on our definition of 'easy' or our child's 'fit' with our own personality and our expectations). If you have a high-needs baby, the struggle to accept your child might be great initially, but overall, loving your baby through his tears can teach you much sooner that all the wishing in the world will not give you a different child. This is unconditional love.

You will also learn compassion, tolerance and flexibility as you meet your baby's needs. These too are strengths to draw on as your child grows. As you attend to his cries, you will discover resources you may never have believed possible: even as you reach the pits of exhaustion, you will gather new reserves of energy. You will learn to recognise when your own reserves are low and when you need nurturing yourself – you will learn to take care of yourself as you take care of your child, because you will be forced to.

A crying baby will teach you to prioritise: you will learn that people matter much more than 'things'. As you sit and rock your baby, instead of becoming restless about that unfinished 'work', look deeply into those trusting navy-blue eyes and ask yourself how much these things would matter if your child were taken from you tomorrow.

100 *As you sit and rock your baby, instead of becoming restless about unfinished 'work', look deeply into those trusting navy-blue eyes and ask yourself how much these things would matter if your child were taken from you tomorrow.*

Mostly, by responding to your crying baby you will have an opportunity to heal yourself: to overcome your own feelings that crying is unhealthy, and perhaps to make a connection with your child that you may have missed out on yourself if your own parents were discouraged from holding you close as you cried. And as you hold your baby close in the dark of night, remember too you are not alone: out there, in another home, in another street, across the world even, another mother will also be holding her own baby close. Through your baby's cries, you are connected through time and space to mothers everywhere.

Resources

Allergies and food intolerance

Allergy Free
www.allergyfree.com.au
Information and support; tips on creating an allergy-free household; personal and baby products available online.

Food Intolerance Network of Australia (FINA)
www.fedupwithfoodadditives.info
Sue Dengate, author of books on allergies and food intolerance, including *Fed Up* and *The Failsafe Cookbook*, offers a wealth of information and resources including a list of food additives, articles, parent stories, links and a free newsletter.

Breastfeeding

Australian Breastfeeding Association
(03) 9885 0855
www.breastfeeding.asn.au

Breastfeeding helplines (24 hours)
ACT & Southern New South Wales: (02) 6258 8928
New South Wales: (02) 9639 8686
Northern Territory: (08) 8411 0301
Queensland: (07) 3844 8977 or (07) 3844 8166
South Australia: (08) 8411 0050
Tasmania: (03) 6223 2609
Victoria: (03) 9885 0653
Western Australia: (08) 9340 1200

Lactation Consultants Association (ALCA)
(02) 6295 0384
www.alca.asn.au
Health professionals offering breastfeeding advice and information. Many hospitals have midwives who are certified lactation consultants. There are also private lactation consultants who offer home visits.

World Health Organization
www.who.int
Up-to-date information about child health, including baby weight and growth charts based on breastfed babies.

Gastric reflux

Distressed Infants Support Association (DISA) of Vic. Inc.
(03) 9786 8568

Vomiting Infants Association of Queensland
(07) 3229 1090
info@reflux.org.au
www.reflux.org.au

Vomiting Infants Support Association (VISA) of New South Wales
(02) 4324 7062

Massage

Gentle Beginnings baby massage DVD
www.pinkymckay.com.au
Presented by certified infant massage instructor Pinky McKay,

this instructional DVD for parents and professional includes full baby massage, mini massage, colic relief strokes, massaging older babies and covers safety, oils, and introducing massage respectfully, with love.

Infant Massage Australia
(03) 9486 4667
www.infantmassage.org.au
Directory of instructors and links to international sites.

Multiple birth

Australian Multiple Birth Association Inc
1300 88 64 99
secretary@amba.org.au
www.amba.org.au

Music for relaxation

Music for Dreaming
info@soundimpressions.com.au
www.musicfordreaming.com/
Classical music played by members of the Melbourne Symphony Orchestra in one continuous piece in ¾ rhythm – the natural rhythm of the human heartbeat; it's used in many hospital nurseries and intensive care units.

Peacebaby
www.peacebaby.com.au
Gentle, relaxing music for mother and baby. Its tempo of 60 beats per minute encourages a deep, even and relaxed breathing pattern.

Sounds for Silence
www.soundsforsilence.com.au
Created in conjunction with a paediatrician, this blend of daily sounds is layered with physiological maternal sounds and white noise to distract, settle and soothe babies.

Parenting information and support

Parent helplines
ACT & New South Wales: 132 055
Queensland & Northern Territory: 1300 301 300
South Australia: 1300 364 100
Tasmania: 1800 808 178
Victoria: 132 289
Western Australia: 1800 654 432 or (08) 9272 1466

Raising Children Network
http://raisingchildren.net.au
This website, supported by the Australian Government, includes a wide range of information about child health, development and behaviour.

Playgroup Associations

www.playgroupaustralia.com.au

New South Wales
1800 171 882 or (02) 9604 5513
admin@playgroupnsw.com.au
www.playgroupnsw.com.au

Northern Territory
Playgroup House Darwin
1800 171 882 or (08) 8945 7775
playgroupnt@octa4.net.au
Playgroup House Alice Springs
(08) 8953 4496

Queensland
1800 171 882 or (07) 3367 2522
info@playgroupqld.com.au

South Australia
1800 171 882 or (08) 8346 2722
info@playgroupsa.com.au

Tasmania
1800 171 882 or (03) 6228 0362
playgrouptas@vision.net.au

Victoria
(03) 9388 1599
pgvic@playgroup.org.au
www.playgroup.org.au

Western Australia
1800 171 882
hotline@playgroupwa.com.au
www.playgroupwa.com.au

Poisoning

Poisons Lifeline
131 114

Postnatal depression

Beyond Blue
www.beyondblue.org.au/postnataldepression

Dona Maria Postnatal Support Network
1300 555 578

Lisa Fettling
0407 943 938
www.lisafettling.com.au
Postnatal depression counsellor, Lisa Fetling is author of *Postnatal Depression: A practical guide for Australian families*, and *Women's Experience of Postnatal Depression*: Kitchen table conversations. Lisa offers individual, group, couple and family counselling and home visits in the Melbourne area. Lisa's website includes information about Postnatal Depression and her services.

Northern Queensland Postnatal Distress Support Group
(07) 4728 1911
tsvpnd@bigpond.com
www.nqpostnataldistress.com

PaNDa (Post and Ante Natal Depression Association Inc) (Victoria)
(03) 9428 4600
www.panda.org.au

Postnatal Disorders Clinic, Mercy Hospital for Women
(03) 9270 2501 or (03) 9270 2884

Post and Antenatal Depression Support and Information (ACT)
(02) 6232 6664
info@pandsi.org.au
www.pandsi.org.au

Postnatal Depression Support Association (Western Australia)
(08) 9340 1622
pndsa@hotmail.com

Premature babies

Austprem
austprem@austprem.org.au
www.austprem.org.au
Internet-based support group for families experiencing the complex challenges of parenting a premature infant.

Bonnie Babes Foundation
(03) 9800 0322
www.bbf.org.au
Telephone, individual and group counselling for miscarriage, prematurity, stillbirth and neonatal loss.

National Premmie Foundation
http://www.prembaby.org.au
A national body of support services with links to Australian premature baby support groups.

Sleep accessories

Babes in Arms
1300 725 276
www.babesinarms.com.au
Babes in Arms is a family business dedicated to helping families choose the most suitable baby carrier for their lifestyle, and are the Australian and New Zealand distributors of the ERGObaby carrier and Peanut Shell.

Mothers' Direct
1800 032 926 (credit card orders)
East Malvern, Melbourne: (03) 9886 9399
Castle Hill, Sydney: (02) 8853 4900
Coorparoo, Brisbane: (07) 3847 5187
www.mothersdirect.com.au
The Australian Breastfeeding Association's retail shops (in Melbourne, Sydney and Brisbane as well as online) are a great place to buy slings. They also sell the Arm's Reach co-sleeper bed in bassinette and cot sizes.

Safe T Sleep
www.safetsleep.com
A patented wrap – useful for reflux babies to prevent sliding down when head of cot is elevated, or to prevent falls from a bed.

Winterwood baby veils
(03) 9879 0426
www.winterwoodtoys.com.au
As well as Steiner-inspired natural baby toys and accessories, Winterwood sells a selection of blue and pink silk veils to place one over the other to create a mauve that surrounds the baby's cradle, softening the room in the early weeks.

Sudden Infant Death Syndrome (SIDS)

National SIDS Council of Australia Ltd
(03) 9819 4595
national@sidsandkids.org
www.sidsaustralia.org.au

New Zealand resources

La Leche League New Zealand
(04) 471 0690
www.lalecheleague.org/LLLNZ

Parents Centre
(04) 476 6950
Offers parents education and support on breastfeeding, infant massage, caesarean birth and miscarriage, and playgroups. Its magazine is *Kiwi Parent*.

Royal New Zealand Plunket Society
(04) 471 0177 or 0800 933 922 (24 hours)
plunket@plunket.org.nz
www.plunket.org.nz

Other websites

Ask Dr Sears
www.askdrsears.com
Attachment parenting guru William Sears and his sons (all paediatricians) offer evidence-based information about all aspects of parenting, including co-sleeping.

Association for Pre- and Perinatal Psychology and Health (APPAH)

www.birthpsychology.com

Attachment Parenting International

www.attachmentparenting.org

Educational materials, research information, consultative, referral and speaker services to promote parenting practices that create strong, healthy emotional bonds between children and their parents. These practices nurture a child's need for trust, empathy, and affection, providing a lifelong foundation for healthy, enduring relationships.

Centre for Attachment

www.centreforattachment.com

A New Zealand-based agency providing support, education, information and training for parents and professionals on optimal child development and attachment. Grounded in research, CFA translates the findings from neuroscience, mental health and psychology to everyday life situations such as mother–infant bonding, feeding and sleeping, family development and relationship health.

Kangaroo Care

www.kangaroomothercare.com

A method of care for all newborns, but in particular for premature babies, with three components: skin-to-skin contact; exclusive breastfeeding; support to the mother–infant dyad.

Pinky McKay

www.pinkymckay.com.au

(Yes this is my site!) Books and DVDs as well as informative articles and links to breastfeeding, health and nurturing sites and a discussion forum. Contact by email is welcome, but I am unable to offer health-related information by email – a personal consultation with a relevant health provider is recommended.

Professor James McKenna
www.nd.edu/~jmckenn1/lab

Professor McKenna (director of the Mother–Baby Behavioural Sleep Lab at the University of Notre Dame, Indiana) is an acclaimed expert in the areas of infant sleep, breastfeeding and Sudden Infant Death Syndrome (SIDS).

Sarah J Buckley
www.sarahjbuckley.com

Author of *Gentle Birth, Gentle Mothering*, GP Sarah Buckley provides inspiring and meticulously researched articles on birth and parenting, including sleep.

Web pages

Australian standards and recommendations for cots
http://www.consumer.gov.au/babysafe/housecots.html

The Australian Association of Infant Mental Health Policy Statement on Controlled Crying
www.aaimhi.org/documents/position%20papers/controlled_crying.pdf

UNICEF UK, Sharing a bed with your baby
www.babyfriendly.org.uk/parents/sharingbed.asp

Further reading

Baldwin Dancy, Rahima, *You Are Your Child's First Teacher*, Celestial Arts, Berkeley, 2000.

Bishop, Lara, *Postnatal Depression: Families in Turmoil*, Halstead Press, Sydney, 1999.

Brodribb, W. (ed.), *Breastfeeding Management*, Australian Breastfeeding Association, Melbourne, 2004.

Buckley, S. J., *Gentle Birth, Gentle Mothering: The Wisdom and Science of Gentle Choices in Pregnancy, Birth, and Parenting*, One Moon Press, Brisbane, 2005.

Campbell, Don, *The Mozart Effect For Children*, Hodder Headline, Sydney, 2000.

Cox, S., *Breastfeeding with Confidence*, Finch Publishing, Sydney, 2004.

Dengate, S., *Fed Up with ADHD*, Random House, Sydney, 2004.

Fettling, Lisa, *Postnatal Depression: A Practical Guide for Australian Families*, IP Communications, Melbourne, 2002.

Heller, S., *The Vital Touch*, Henry Holt and Company, New York, 1997.

Jackson, D., *Three in a Bed*, Bloomsbury, London, 1999.

Kitzinger, Sheila, *Understanding Your Crying Baby*, Lothian, Melbourne, 2005.

La Leche League International, *The Womanly Art of Breastfeeding* (sixth edition), Plume, New York, 1997.

Le Blanc, Wendy, *Naked Motherhood*, Random House, Sydney, 1999.

Masi, Dr Wendy S. & Cohen Leiderman, Dr Roni, *Baby Play: Gymboree*, Weldon Owen Publishing, California, 2001.

McKay, P. *Sleeping Like a Baby*, Penguin, Melbourne, 2006.

McKenna, James J., *Sleeping With Your Baby*, Platypus Media, Washington DC, 2007.

Minchin, M., *Is Your Baby Sleeping Safely?*, Baby Friendly, Melbourne, 2004.

Mohrbacher, N. & Stock, J. *Breastfeeding Answer Book* (revised edition), La Leche League International, Illinois, 1997.

Odent M., *Primal Health*, Clairview, London, 2002.

—— *The Scientification of Love*, Free Association Books, London, 2001.

Sears, W., *Nighttime Parenting: How to Get Your Baby and Child to Sleep*, La Leche League International, Illinois, 1999.

Solter, Aletha, *The Aware Baby*, Shining Star Press, Goleta, 1984.

Sunderland, M., *The Science of Parenting*, DK, London, 2006.

Vanderijt, H. & Plooij, F., *The Wonder Weeks: How to Turn Your Baby's Eight Great Fussy Phases into Magical Leaps Forward*, Kiddy World Promotions, USA, 2003.

Acknowledgements

Many thanks to all the amazingly dedicated (and honest) parents who shared their crying baby stories: from you, others will learn that it 'isn't their fault' that their baby cries (and cries!).

Thank you to all the midwives, lactation consultants and childbirth educators who helped find these voices and shared their concern, information and support during the writing of *100 Ways to Calm the Crying*, especially: Barb Glare; Jane Palmer; Julia Monaghan; Jane Myers; Barbara Ash; Margaret Callaghan; Ruth Cantrill; Lina Clerke; Heidi McWilliam; Erika Munton; infant-massage instructor Jeanette Miller and Dr Sarah Buckley, GP

Thanks also to the wonderful publishers and editors at Penguin, especially Kirsten Abbott and Miriam Cannell, and to my agent Jacinta DiMase, who have kept this book 'out there' for distressed parents and babies.

Index

Sleeping
Like a Baby

Are you obsessed about your baby's sleep?

Do you feel 'weak' because you can't bear to leave him to cry himself to asleep?

Do you need to relax more and enjoy being a parent?

Parenting expert Pinky McKay offers a natural, intuitive approach to solving your little ones' sleep problems and gives practical tips on how to:

★ understand your baby's tired cues

★ create a safe sleeping environment

★ gently settle babies and toddlers

★ feed infants to encourage sleep

'Scientific, holistic and heart-centred insights into infant sleep, settling and bonding.'

Lauren Porter, BA, MSW. Co-director, Centre for Attachment